Scrapbooking

FOR HOME DÉCOR

Scrapbooking

FOR HOME DÉCOR

How to Create Frames, Boxes,
and Other Beautiful Items from
Photographs and Family Memories

CANDICE WINDHAM

Design
Originals

an Imprint of Fox Chapel Publishing
www.d-originals.com

Keepsake Sewing Box, page 76.

ISBN 978-1-57421-411-6

Library of Congress Cataloging-in-Publication Data

Windham, Candice.
 Scrapbooking for home décor / by Candice Windham. -- First [edition].
     pages cm
 Includes index.
   ISBN 978-1-57421-411-6 (pbk.)
 1. Handicraft. 2. Souvenirs (Keepsakes) 3. Photographs--Trimming, mounting, etc. 4. Photographs in interior decoration. I. Title.
 TT857.W56 2012
 745.5--dc23
                         2012014126

Printed in China
First Printing

About the Author

Born and raised in Memphis, Tennessee, Candice Windham is an award-winning graphic designer and fine artist, working in watercolor, acrylics, colored pencil and paper, and altered arts.

Her earliest memories include drawing, clay modeling, and crafting with her younger sister, Lynn, and her grandmother, who, along with the rest of the family, always encouraged their artistic endeavors.

Windham is the owner of Windham Design Studio, providing design, layout, and illustration for a variety of printed materials, as well as display design for various trade shows. She also is curator and designer of the Memphis Light, Gas, and Water Historical Museum.

Her work has been published in a variety of paper arts and crafts magazines and books, and she is an instructor in rubber-stamping, scrapbooking, mixed media acrylic collage, and altered arts.

Candice Windham, her husband, Larry, and son, Michael, along with pups, Pete and Sam, reside in Brighton, Tennessee.

Dedication

This book is dedicated to the memory of my wonderful family and to my husband, Larry, and son, Michael, who have always believed in me.

Can Full of Memories, page 64.

Contents

What You Can Make

Memories in Plain Sight

Scrapbooking isn't just for paper anymore!

Wood

Family Tribute Shelf, p. 54

Jewelry Box Storage Caddies, p. 68

Heirloom Stationery Box, p. 72

Textiles

Fabric Photo Wall Hanging, p. 110

Shadow Box Book, p. 90

Behind Glass

Recipe Serving Tray, p. 82

Relationship Wall Art, p. 58

Metal

Can Full of Memories, p. 64

Keepsake Sewing Box, p. 76

Copper Flower Hanger, p. 104

Mixed Media

Birthday Card Book, p. 98

Memory Charm Napkin Rings, p. 86

What You Can Learn From This Book

Bring your cherished memories out of the scrapbook and into plain sight. This book will show you how to create stunning, one-of-a-kind tribute pieces that are both useful and decorative. Any of the nine display pieces, plus three bonus projects, is easily adapted to your own taste and decorating style. You'll learn about tools and materials as well as dozens of tips and techniques.

Tools of the Trade, p. 14

All About Papers, p. 16

Using the Right Adhesive, p. 18

Choosing an Embossing/ Die-Cutting Machine, p. 24

Hardware, p. 24

All About Ink, p. 25

Paint Types, p. 27

Scoring, p. 28

Workshop and Kitchen Tools, p. 30

Cutting Instruments, p. 32

Punches, p. 33

Layering, p. 35

Making Nameplates, p. 36

Rubber Stamping, p. 37

Customizing Background Paper, p. 37

Faux Stitching, p. 38

Aging with Sponging, p. 39

Direct-to-Paper Inking, p. 39

Metal Stamping, p. 40

Mechanical Embossing, p. 42

Embossing Templates, p. 42

Die Cutting, p. 44

Working with Clay, p. 45

Setting Eyelets, p. 46

Using Resin, p. 46

Heat Embossing, p. 47

Batik Embossing, p. 50

Making Knots, p. 51

Making Books, p. 98

Inking on Metal, p. 79

Printing on Fabric, p. 114

Introduction

Mixed-media art has become the rage lately, whether it's on canvas, wood, paper, or just about any other surface available. Websites and television programs have fueled a renewed interest in family history. Combine mixed-media art with family history and you have the basis of a new trend.

Scrapbooking has been around for a long time. I remember making my first scrapbooks using a big, clumsy book with ornery pages that just wouldn't stay put with that little black cord that was supposed to hold it all together. The pages tore easily from the reinforcements, and I continuously had to scoop them up off the floor, with black-gummed photo corners and memorabilia flying everywhere.

The modern scrapbook has come a long way. We have incredible binding options with acid-free, lignin-free materials to protect our precious memories. We travel in a frenzy to our local scrapbook store to get the latest and greatest, gotta-have-it-first tool or paper collection and haul it all to the next big crop, where we proudly show it off to our friends. In six months, the next greatest thing will have replaced it. It's a vicious cycle.

The sad part is we make all of these beautiful layouts, preserving even the tiniest special memory of our families, and very few people ever see them. We purchase huge albums and fill them with photos and memorabilia from our latest vacation, little Mary's piano recital, and all the other major milestones in our lives. What next? We put them in a bookcase or lay them on a coffee table and dust them every so often.

I took an abstract collage/painting class a few years ago, and the instructor asked us to bring photos or newspapers to class to use in our work. I happily cut and tore and pasted words and images into my project. When the instructor came to my table on her hourly tours of the class, she said, "Get rid of the faces. You don't want all those people in there if you can see who they are." I was dumbfounded. I liked the faces. They were family photos that I had copied for this class.

In this book, you will find ideas that, I hope, inspire you to step out of that scrapbook comfort zone and put your memories out there for everyone to see.

The more I thought about it, the more determined I was to use the faces, not send them to oblivion. My first piece was a collage of all the strong women in my life. It received the People's Choice Award in the first competition in which it was entered.

That painting was the first of a series with the same theme: honoring my ancestors. Every time I entered one of these paintings in a competition, I came home with a prize.

Unfortunately, I was working on a very large scale, which is great if you have a very large-scale home or a very large, very wealthy family who clamor to buy your latest works, which I don't. I had to find a way of using my treasured family photos in a smaller way. That's when I turned to crafting.

Crafting has gotten a bad rap over the years. Today's crafters are far more advanced than what we saw fifty years ago, and anyone who can read directions can create some incredible items, especially in home décor.

In this book, you will find ideas that, I hope, inspire you to step out of that scrapbook comfort zone and put your memories out there for everyone to see.

This book also features love stories, black sheep, and keepsakes. Adapt these projects for your own use. Each idea could have several takes, such as the Jewelry Box Storage Caddies (p. 72) or the Can Full of Memories (p. 64).

I hope you'll use these ideas as a springboard to take your memory preservation to a new level. Have fun. I know I did!

Ephemera

Every project in this book can be highly personalized—most are dedication pieces honoring family legacies and favorite memories. The one characteristic that remains constant across the board is ephemera.

Ephemera are things that can only make a project better. While ephemera usually comes in the form of paper, such as book pages (especially in another language), letters, family photos, old bills of lading, greeting cards, labels, etc., it can also be dimensional objects like old keys, tiny bottles, buttons, and more.

Be sure to really think about what you are using, whether there is a renewable source, and whether or not it is valuable, either in monetary terms or sentiment.

If it's the latter, you might want to consider photocopying those love letters between your grandparents and storing the originals in a safe place. Just age the copies with sponged edges or a tea or coffee soak.

Think of all the paper you have around the house. You don't have to destroy a book to use its pages. Just photocopy what you need and put it back on the shelf. Did your mother save every magazine she ever read? They are wonderful sources of ephemera, including the column headlines, which may have just the words you want. Her sewing box could hold treasures such as needle books, buttons on cards (scan and save the original, unless it's fairly

new), machine needle packets, and specialty scissors.

Don't have a lot of old treasures? There are books and CDs on the market to provide you with all the instant ancestors and paper ephemera you will ever need. A trip to the flea market or an estate sale can give up additional material that will have no sentimental value to you, so you can use it freely without guilt.

The sources of ephemera are limitless, and discovering exactly what you are looking for is a pleasure in itself. Happy hunting!

Chapter 1
Tools of the Trade

You can make just about anything if you have the right tools. With so many options on the market, it is easy to buy equipment you really don't need. This chapter shows tools necessary to create all of the projects in this book without going overboard.

Choosing the Right Tools

Having the correct tools can make your crafting so much easier, but beware the gotta-have-it-and-gotta-have-it-now syndrome. You can overload yourself with so many gadgets that seem like such a good idea in the store or when you're surfing online at three in the morning. The result is that you end up with a load of tools you don't really need and have to sort through when you are ready to work. When you're holding two objects joined by quick-dry glue with one hand and trying to find that cute little tool you bought to mop up glue drips with the other, it can lead to utter frustration. Gadgets also require a lot of valuable real estate in your studio.

The following is a review of many of the tools I use and includes those you will need for the projects in upcoming chapters.

Choosing paper.
Choosing the right
papers can turn
ordinary images
into elegant,
art-quality pieces like
Relationship Wall Art
(p. 58).

Paper

There are so many gorgeous types of paper available that you can get lost in a scrapbook store. Using top-quality paper in your projects ensures they will remain beautiful for years to come.

Many papers come in slabs (or stacks), which have anywhere from 12 to 50 sheets of paper, cardstock, and embellishments. They are all coordinated, so it takes the guesswork out of trying to match pieces from different manufacturers. You will also get a break on the price as opposed to purchasing individual sheets.

Lightweight papers are fine for scrapbooking, party favors, etc., but if you want something that will hold up to wear and tear, or if you are going to be scoring and folding, cardstock works best. It has a more substantial feel, and the scoring tool or blade will not cut through it under normal circumstances.

You also need to be careful of your adhesive when attaching thin papers to sturdy surfaces such as a cigar box or metal surface. Unless the glue says *wrinkle-free* on the label, you will probably be unhappy when your project dries. The solution is to either use a spray adhesive, double-stick tape, or an adhesive application machine that spreads a thin coat of double-stick adhesive over the paper.

Single- and double-sided paper is available. They also come in many surface textures and media, including both dry- and heat-embossed surfaces, metallic and pearl finishes, and matte and glossy finishes, so you are only limited by your imagination.

Buying paper

Try to avoid becoming a paper-hoarder with stacks of beautiful paper you flip through like a miser with his gold, never using them for fear that you will never be able to find them should you need more. Trust me. I don't follow my own advice and have just such a stash of paper and I have no idea what possessed me to buy most of it.

There are so many new types of paper coming out every day that what you loved last year will be like fad fashions: They are fun to have for a while, but then they go out of style or you just get tired of them. Then what do you do with them? Resist the urge to buy every design in a coordinated line unless you already have a project in mind for them, then label the collection when you get home, so you can remember what you had planned, and avoid coming across it months later and wondering, "What was I thinking?"

ABOUT PAPER SCRAPS

It's very easy to become a paper scrap hoarder. When I first discovered rubber-stamping, I remember a friend calling to see if I had one company's specific color of yellow cardstock. She needed a piece 1" x 3" (25 x 76mm) and did not want to cut another whole piece of paper. I don't think it ever occurred to her that it would cost five-times that of a new sheet of paper to drive to my house to get the scrap.

Many people fall into the trap of keeping every scrap of paper they ever create. Do they go through their stash when they need the small pieces? *Maybe.* Does it take a lot of time to sort by color or manufacturer and remind yourself to always check the stash? *Definitely.* I became overloaded with scraps until one day I just loaded them all up and took them to a couple of families who had kids who loved crafts. They loved the gift; I loved the free space it created in my studio.

I no longer keep anything smaller than 2½" x 3½" (64 x 89mm), for tags and artist trading cards, and only if I take the time right then to trim them to that size. I also trim scraps to 5½" x 8½" (140 x 216mm) for folded cards and 4" x 5¼" (102 x 133mm) and 3¾" x 5" (95 x 127mm), the two sizes I use most often for layering a card front. That way I know I'll use them eventually. I keep these organized in a small cigar box on my worktable so that I don't forget about them.

Adhesives

I keep a variety of adhesives on hand so that I always have the exact product made for my purpose. There's nothing more heart breaking than having your favorite project fall apart in six months because you used the wrong adhesive.

GLUE STICKS

Glue sticks are the original scrapbook workhorses. If you have a good experience with your first glue stick, you will probably want to use that brand for the rest of your life. Glue sticks are small, lightweight, portable, and don't drip. If you used glue sticks a long time ago and had a bad experience, it will probably take a strong force to convince you to try them again. There have been great strides in glue sticks in the last few years and they are much better now, but remember, you get what you pay for. Getting 10 for $1 is no bargain if they don't hold your project elements in place over time.

SPRAY ADHESIVE

One of my favorite ways to adhere large pieces of paper is spray adhesive. Most spray adhesives remain repositionable for a few seconds. If you want super-permanent adhesion, spray both pieces to be adhered, wait a few minutes, and then press them together.

Be sure to work in a well-ventilated area and protect the surrounding area from overspray. There are spray boxes made for this. I use a small one when spraying small pieces, but the one I recommend is a large cardboard box with the opening turned to the side. Use it until it has a pile of adhesive residue on the bottom, then turn it to a clean side. When you get back to the first dirty side, it has usually dried and you can

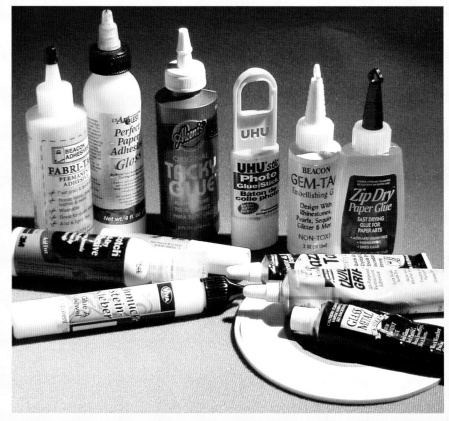

start over. I've been using the same box for more than two years and plan to have it a lot longer.

LIQUID GLUES

Liquid glue is a staple of the craft industry. Glues with trim-off tips are great because you can trim just a little to get a tiny line or trim a little more to get larger distribution.

Able-bodied white adhesives that dry clear are my favorites for adhering cardstock to cardstock and embellishments to just about any surface.

There are also clear, liquid glues that work very well with paper-to-paper applications as well as a host of products for fabric and jewelry.

Adhesives. A variety of adhesives are available depending on the job they need to perform and the media used in a project.

CLEAR-DRYING CAULK

Clear-drying caulk isn't my adhesive of choice for paper projects, but it does have its use in the studio. If you need a watertight seal on anything, small tubes of bath and kitchen caulk work wonders. I use them for sealing the edges around a piece of glass or thick acrylic sheeting when making custom serving trays.

REPOSITIONABLE ADHESIVES

When you're trying to adhere something, why in the world would you need repositionable adhesives? The term alone suggests instability, but there are many uses for this product. It works great when using stencils, keeping them in place while you add paint or ink. If you are unsure about your scrapbook layout, use repositionable adhesive on the photos and change them out or move them around until you are happy with the results.

TAPE

Double-stick tape: The invention of double-stick tape for the craft industry makes it so easy to place items where you want them and get really good adhesion, especially along edges such as layers on greeting cards or scrapbook pages. You can get double-stick (or double-sided) tape on rolls that require cutting with scissors, small dispensers that are great for on-the-go crafting, and large tape guns that hold big rolls of the tape width of your choice. You can also find heavy-duty, double-stick tape in sheets, approximately 6" x 8" (152 x 203mm).

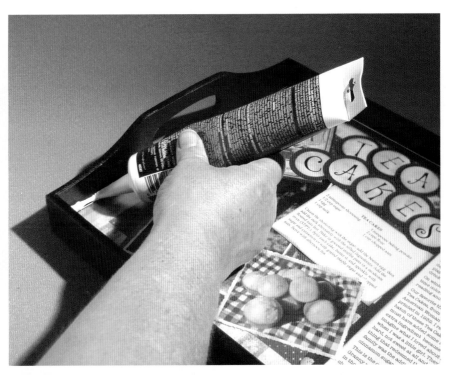

Edge sealing. Use waterproof, clear-drying caulk for sealing the edges around a piece of glass or thick acrylic sheeting when making custom serving trays (p. 82).

Masking tape: Use masking tape to temporarily hold two pieces together when waiting for glue to dry. When paired with a permanent marker, it also makes great labels for items in your studio, such as drawers, which can contain lots of different items.

Book tape: I love book tape. It is made of fine-quality linen that feels like canvas, so it can be painted, inked, or stamped. You can use it as it was designed to reinforce the binding of an old book, but also for creating new books, such as the *Birthday Card Book* (p. 98), as well as new elements for your projects like the hinges for the cigar box in the *Heirloom Stationery Box* project (p. 72).

HOT GLUE

Hot glue is great for three-dimensional projects that require adhesion between several surfaces. You can get low-temperature glue sticks and guns that do not require as much heat as the original style, but still hold well. You always run the risk of burning yourself with dripping glue or when trying to reassemble a fallen embellishment before the glue dries.

Terrific tips

After you have completed your project using hot glue, there may be some stray stings of glue hanging around. Use your hair dryer to remove them. Just turn it on, aim the blower at the project, and the strings will fly away.

Bases

Bases are the objects we use as a beginning to our projects. They include metal, cigar, and papier-mâché boxes, trays, books, shelves, jewelry boxes, picture frames, and cans. I'm sure you can think of many more.

Many objects can become the basis of an art project, so be sure to think twice before you throw out that old tin or frame. The addition of a new coat of paint and a few embellishments can make it a family heirloom.

Discard? Any item is a potential base for displaying memories and, because it will be covered, it doesn't have to be brand new.

Distressing Tools

There are a lot of ways to create a vintage or distressed appearance for your work.

Sanding. Just scrub sandpaper, a sanding block, or emery boards over your paper or painted items, especially along the edges, to create a worn look. Combine the technique with ink sponging for even more possibilities.

Specialty tools. There are a lot of these on the market and more coming daily. You can get tools with small, sturdy wires on the end to rough up surfaces and tool kits with metal file blades made to get into small places. Some are round disks, through which you slide your paper's edges back and forth to distress.

Adding nostalgia. Aging techniques add nostalgia to projects and are easy to create with specialty tools or simple sandpaper.

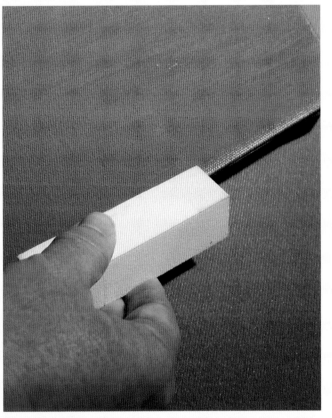

Simulating wear. Gently sanding painted edges simulates years of wear.

Terrific tips

Don't have an army of distressing tools at your fingertips? The blades of your scissors can substitute. Just hold the scissors open and run the sharp edge of the blade back and forth along the edge of your paper.

Also, try tearing the edges for another distressed look. Tear, pulling the torn scrap paper toward you, to get the white edges of the base paper showing, or away from you to keep the top color showing.

Embellishments

Personalizing. Embellishments can include just about anything from books to buttons, childhood treasures, or keepsakes.

Embellishments give our work a finished, pushing-the-envelope appearance.

There are a ton of embellishments on the market and if you look hard enough, you can find anything you are looking for, from apples to zebras, paper to fabric, and stickers to die cuts. Want to save some money? Look around your house for things you might already have on hand.

THE SEWING BASKET

The sewing basket holds a wealth of embellishments, from pins and needles and thread to zippers, which can be used to reveal something on a scrapbook page or rolled and secured with stitching to create a gorgeous rose. Use an old tape measure to add interest to a custom sewing container or metal snaps to glue on a project just for the sake of adding a little texture. Don't forget the buttons! There could be an entire book written on the creative uses of buttons!

BEADS

Beads aren't just for dressing up your apparel anymore. They are perfect to add a little bling to a project with bright, spicy colors or dress it down with subdued colors that have the look and feel of pebbles.

Microbeads are just what they claim to be. They are very tiny and make beautiful embellishments. Cover the surface of a photo or any printed image with clear-drying adhesive and pour on clear microbeads to create a beautiful, shimmery embellishment or frame it for custom art.

OLD BOOKS

Old books are great, especially dictionaries or foreign language text. Pages can be used as a background or for journaling. Be sure they aren't valuable editions before you tear, rip, and paint to your heart's content. Add a resin coating and you have permanent, waterproof paper. The color of the page will intensify and make great embellishments for indoor or outdoor projects.

JUNK PHOTOS

In the days before instant gratification with digital cameras, there was the point, shoot, and wait camera. You never knew what you had until the photo-processing lab finished with them. Nine times out of ten, you had a few blurry shots, ugly shots, or pictures of your feet that were accidents.

All is not entirely lost. Cut them into 1" (25mm) squares and reassemble in a random pattern. Mosaics make lovely tags or trims. Or, try rubber-stamping on blurry photos with permanent ink. The colors provide an instant background and create beautiful embellishments out of bad photos.

TRAVEL BROCHURES

Every time we stop at a welcome center in our travels, I pick up brochures, maps, and other printed materials. I usually use these items (sprayed with a deacidification spray first!) in scrapbook pages, but I always have leftovers. They can become background papers for home décor projects. Tint maps with inks, dye spritzers, tea, or coffee. Crumple them while wet, then spread out to dry. Use an inkpad to lightly brush over the surface. The ink emphasizes wrinkles and you will have a lovely piece of original art.

OLD CALENDARS AND CARDS

The art calendar and greeting card business just gets bigger every day. You can find everything from cartoons to fine art. These can be used as background images or become custom art.

OTHER EMBELLISHMENTS

Bottle caps. Bottle caps can be flattened and painted for a flower effect. Turn them over, glue in a photo, and fill them with resin or embossing powder. You have instant 3-D embellishments or add a magnet for fridge décor.

Seed packets. After you've planted your garden, keep those seed packets with their fabulous art. They are great for greeting cards, scrapbook pages, or, when covered with a sealant, outdoor projects, such as a flower pot for your patio table.

Pencils and crayons. Use short pencils, approximately 4" (102mm) long to make a fence for a card, a 3-D object such as a birdhouse, or a scrapbook page. Just give them a splash of paint and glue them, evenly spaced, to two thin strips of mat board, top and bottom. These make a great embellishment for the base of a flowerpot or paint can.

Crayons can be added to beeswax projects for additional color. They can also be melted and used in bottle caps with a wick to create tiny votive candles.

Floral pebbles. Remember that bag of clear or colored pebbles you used in your flowers for that last party? Pull them out and put them to work. Glue a photo or patterned paper face-up on the flat side with clear-drying adhesive. Add a magnet and you have fridge décor. Glue them on a project for texture or emphasis.

Create sparkle. Beads make beautiful embellishments and come in nearly every color imaginable.

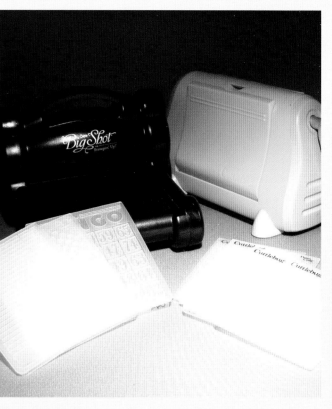

Sophistication. Die cuts add a touch of sophistication because of their intricate details. They also create dimension when layered with photos or other die cuts. Just about any subject, any shape, can be found in die-cut templates, from simple circles to elaborate pieces that pop up when opened.

Machine aid.
Hand-crank machines take the work out of die cutting and embossing.

Elegance. Adding gold paint to hardware creates elegant legs for the *Heirloom Stationery Box* (p. 72).

(p. 72).

Terrific tips

Dye inks are not suitable for embossing because they dry too quickly. The only exception is Ranger Distress Ink Pads.

Embossing & die cutting. There are many embossing and die-cutting machines on the market so it can be hard to determine which is right for you. I solved the problem by purchasing four: one for large dies and mat board, one for paper texturizing, one for die-cut letters, and one for custom cutting. Had I been patient, I could have saved myself some money and worktop space by doing a little research. My large die-cutting machine, with a little adaptability, will do the work of two of the others.

Texture plates are just what they say: They add texture to paper, cardstock, and thin metals. Some are made like little folders in which you place your material, close the folder, and run it through your embossing machine. These are limited to the size of the folder, although you can maneuver the paper to cover more area in some cases.

Use larger texture plates with a paper stump and stylus. They take longer, but the larger image is worth the effort. They can also be run through some embossing machines.

Hardware. Hardware stores are my favorite places to shop for things like hinges, drawer pulls, filigree corners, and toolboxes. Just spend a morning rummaging through your local hardware emporium and see what you come up with to add interest to your projects.

Inks

The wealth of types and colors from inkpads and liquid inks is sometimes overwhelming. If you know a few simple properties, you can be sure to use ink that will give you the results you want. Inkpads should be stored upside down so that the pad stays moist. Inkpads that are already upside down when you close the lid should be stored with the lid side up.

DYE INKS

Dye inks are the basic ink for rubber-stamping. They come in every color of the rainbow, so you are sure to get what you need. Be careful you don't wind up with so many colors that you feel swamped with choices and then always end up using black or brown for everything.

Dye inks can be used for most stamping techniques, including basic stamping, direct-to-paper, sponging, and edging (see Chapter 2, p.37). They can be re-inked, so they last a long time.

Selecting ink. Inks are specially made to add color and dimension to paper, wood, fabric, or metal.

You can also close the lid of the pad, squeeze so that the lid comes in contact with the inked pad and use the ink residue in the lid like watercolor paint. Just wet your brush and touch it lightly to the ink residue, then use the color to add shading or tinting to your project. Using the residue in the lid keeps you from diluting your inkpad.

PIGMENT INKS

Pigment inks take longer to dry than dye inks. As a result, they can be used with embossing powder for heat embossing (p. 47). They are also effective when you need a light-colored stamp on dark paper. They contain chalk, which makes them more opaque than dye inks.

Pigment inks are permanent when dry, so they can be used for outline stamps and colored with alcohol or dye inks without fear of colors bleeding. Pigment inkpads can also be re-inked.

Keeping memories safe

The scrapbooks from years ago all have a brown edge surrounding the pages. This is a very desirable look and one I love to fake in my work, but the real thing is dangerous to your photos and cherished papers or letters. That brown edge is a sign that acid is eating away at your memories.

If you want to use printed paper, such as travel brochures or maps, and don't know if they are acid-free, spray them front and back with a deacidification spray first. This prevents any acid in the paper from creeping in to your scrapbooks or memory projects.

If you plan to use items such as newspaper articles or photos that are printed on paper you can't confirm as acid-free, my advice is to have color copies made of the these items or scan and reprint them on your own printer, use them in your projects, and store the originals in an acid-free environment. If you don't know for sure that the copy paper or printer paper is acid free, spray it.

ALCOHOL INKS

Alcohol inks are just what they say. They come in small bottles with dropper tips, are alcohol-based, dry quickly, and can be used on a lot of surfaces, including metal and glass.

There are tools available for applying alcohol inks, like those used in creating the brilliant colors on the *Copper Flower Hanger* (p. 104). Included are handled felt and sponges as well as empty markers that can be filled with your choice of inks or ink combinations for custom colors. A small sponge or piece of felt will also work as an inexpensive applicator.

CLEAR EMBOSSING INKS

The clear embossing pad is one of my favorite inkpads. You can stamp an image and then emboss it (p. 47) with a heat tool, or add mica powder. The powder only adheres to the ink, so you end up with a beautiful stamped image with the shimmer of mica.

You can substitute a small coffee warmer, iron, or old griddle for a heat tool, but heat tools are so inexpensive (generally under $20) that it is worth the investment. With the other heating elements, you have to lay the paper on the hot surface (this means turning the iron upside down), then move it around until all of the powder melts. It takes more time than using a heat tool and

Accents. Deep veins stand out on the gold-painted leaves in the *Copper Plant Hanger* (p. 104) when accented with alcohol ink.

your time is more valuable than $20. A note of caution: When using powder, you cannot substitute a hair dryer for a heat tool, no matter how hot it becomes. The hair dryer will just blow the powder away.

Measuring Tools

You can't create without a ruler, no matter how much of an out-of-the-box designer you are. The old-fashioned wooden ruler and yardstick have been around forever, but they weren't made for getting a good, straight cut using a craft knife. You will eventually have a ruler that is only good for creating jagged, wavy lines or one that is stained and finds a home in one of your projects.

Some rulers are metal and measure in inches, centimeters, and picas. Some have magnets on the back and, when used with the matching metal-core craft mat, keep you on the straight and narrow. There are see-through rulers and acrylic rulers with metal-edged cutting guides. Buy the best you can afford. It will last you forever and you'll

be glad you paid a little extra for a metal or metal-edged ruler.

It's also a good idea to spring for a metal T-square. I have several wooden T-squares with acrylic edges, but always wonder if they are square. My favorite is a 36" (915mm) metal T-square that I use for cutting mats and trimming long, straight lines on fabric and paper.

Triangles are perfect for getting a 90° or 45° cut. I prefer the acrylic triangles, which have rulers etched in the acrylic and metal edges for trimming. These are great for cutting small papers quickly and aligning elements in your work.

Accuracy vital. Accurate measurements are vital when cutting papers and photographs.

Proper brush. Having the correct brush for the job makes a difference in the quality of the finished product.

Paint

Paint can make an old object new again. It can liven up the color in a drab room. There are many different paints on the market today, and it is easy to be overwhelmed with the selections available.

- Water-based paints are the most popular, simply for the ease of clean up.

- Acrylics come in transparent, semi-transparent, and opaque colors.

- Watercolor is still a great way to add color to a stamped image.

- Metallic water-based paints, which come in liquids and pens, can really add pizzazz to a project.

- Dimensional paints hold their shape in small quantities, such as adding lines or dots, or they can be built up to create depth, such as creating a faux bezel.

- Markers have come a long way from the standard black markers of the 1950s. Now they are available in every color of the rainbow and some brands even make markers and stamp pads in the same colors.

- Spray paint is one of my favorite mediums. I love the color variety and the endless list of special effects. One of my favorite items to spray paint is mat board whether it is an actual mat or a die cut. I always spray any three-dimensional die cut to cover the white core of the mat board.

Paint's role. Like inks, paints are made for covering specific surfaces and creating certain effects.

Metallic paints. Metallic water-based paints, which come in liquids or pens, really add pizzazz to projects such as the lid for the *Can Full of Memories* (p. 64).

PAINTBRUSHES

Having the correct brush can make a big difference in your painted project. Bristle brushes, which are great for acrylics, turn watercolor into a mess, but you don't want to use your fine sable watercolor brushes with acrylics unless you are prepared to spend the time necessary to really clean them. For craft projects, inexpensive foam brushes as well as student-grade brushes are fine. If the paint happens to get dry in an inexpensive brush, just toss it and get a new one.

Terrific tips

Clean your brush as soon as possible after a watercolor or acrylic painting session. If you must delay a proper cleanup until later, place the brush in water, but remember, if you leave it there too long, the hairs (or bristles) will become curved from the water as well as the weight of the handle. You can straighten them out, but it takes time and patience.

When you clean your brush, use warm, soapy water and especially massage the area where the hairs are joined into the ferrule. Rinse well and lay aside to dry. Never store a wet brush with the hairs at the top. The water will eventually rot the brush hair, which will end up in your project, probably at the most inopportune time.

Score then fold. Crisp, clean folds are easily achieved when papers are scored first.

If you accidently have your score at a bit of an angle, the edges won't line up when you make the fold. To remedy this, place your folded paper on your paper trimmer. Using the fold as your straight guide, trim the smallest amount possible from the other three sides to get an even rectangle.

If you don't have a bone folder, you can use an old ballpoint pen, preferably non-working, a wooden skewer, or a very dull pencil to score the fold line. You may get pencil or ink residue on your paper. Erase the pencil mark or cover the area with a scrap of patterned paper to hide the ink marks.

Scoring Tools

Scoring makes it possible to fold any paper where you want it to fold. Paper has a grain, just like wood. Fold with the grain and you have a beautiful edge. Fold against the grain and you have a mess, with jagged edges. When you score paper and cardstock, the scoring blade breaks down the fibers of the paper and makes the fold perfect, no matter what the grain.

BONE FOLDERS

The world of crafting got much easier when the bone folder was introduced. This little stick, which looks like a fat Popsicle stick with a rounded point on one end, can make your paper folds neat and crisp.

Using a ruler, place the edge along the area where you want the fold with the reverse side of the paper face up. Draw the pointed end of the bone folder along the straight edge and fold. Use the side of the bone folder to smooth the fold and make it sharp.

PAPER TRIMMERS

Some paper trimmers come with a scoring blade or have them available for purchase. These work just fine, especially for small projects.

SCORING BOARDS

There are a variety of scoring boards on the market. If you like to make cards and make a lot of them, this tool is a necessity. It has a ruler at the top and a small metal strip with tracks on either side down the middle. Just position your paper with the point where you want the fold at 0 on the top of the board and use the special tool that comes with it to create your scoring line. It also makes a perfect accordion-folded piece. Just position each fold point at 0 and make the score, but remember to flip the paper from back to front for each consecutive fold.

Sponges

Applying color with sponges is a great way to create texture, add color quickly, or tint two different sheets of printed paper or cardstock so that the colors will work as a cohesive unit on your project. You can apply ink, paint, or chalk with sponges—they are very versatile tools.

Makeup sponges work well, but also can leave a hard edge if you aren't careful. Small, round sponges available at craft and scrapbook stores can be cut like a pie into eight pieces.

My sponge of choice is a grout sponge, available from home improvement stores for about $3 for a 6" x 4" x 2"

(152 x 102 x 51mm) sponge. Cut these into many small pieces, about 1" x 2" (25 x 51mm). The edges of the sponge are curved and make the best impressions.

If you want to be thrifty, collect your used sponges until you have used up most of your grout sponge stash, throw them in an old sock or piece of hosiery, and toss them into the laundry with your dark colors. Lay them out in the sun to air dry. The result won't be as bright as the original sponges, but they will be clean and ready to use again. See *Techniques*, Chapter 2 (p. 39), for sponge uses and effects.

Sponges. When used to apply color, the porous nature of sponges produces subtle differences in intensity and dimension.

Surface Protection

I like to imagine myself as a very neat designer, with everything organized and no mistakes ever. Ha! The truth is you can hardly use glue, paint, inks, etc., without getting them everywhere, especially on your work surface.

There are many surface protectors on the market. I rely on four: the craft mat, waxed paper, waste paper, and the cutting mat.

CRAFT MAT

This tool was originally designed for bakers to line their cookie sheets. They have a non-stick surface and some have a slightly sticky backside so they don't slide around on your worktable.

You can drip paint, ink, and glue on them and wipe it right off. You can also use them as an art tool, dripping liquid colors or spraying colored mists, then pressing your paper to the surface. The result is a wonderful mingling of colors,

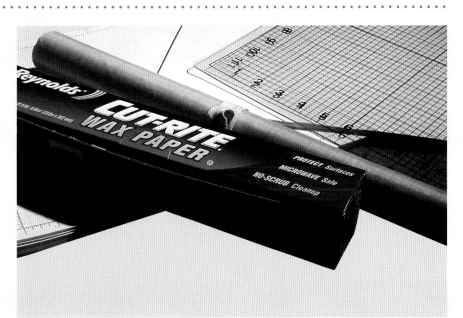

Keep it clean. Protecting surfaces is easy when using a couple of purchased mats and common household products and refuse.

which is hard to create with traditional brushes or other applicators.

WAXED PAPER

It's not just for school lunches anymore! Waxed paper is a great surface protector when you need something temporary, but is also perfect for transporting a flat, not-quite-dry project. Just put waxed paper between the pages of a book or between scrapbook page sheets. The piece will be protected until you are at a place where you can lay it out to finish drying.

WASTE PAPER

Waste paper is very easy to come by when you think about it.

- Every time you purchase a fragile item at a store, they wrap it in paper. Roll the used paper around a mailing tube or a cardboard wrapping paper roll to store and just pull off a new sheet as needed.

- When you place an online order, the shipper uses paper to fill excess space in the shipping box. The paper is usually very long and is perfect for covering your entire work surface to protect it from messy applications.

- When you get a new telephone book, you have an old one waiting to be discarded. This is the perfect surface when you need to over-glue the edges so that the glue covers the entire element. When the book page gets sticky, just turn to another. Be sure to watch for ink transfer, especially if you are working on light-colored cardstock.

- Newspaper is my least favorite of the waste papers because the ink is so fresh and can easily transfer, but it's still great for using under projects for spray painting.

CUTTING SURFACES

Cutting mats are self-healing and allow you to make deep cuts with a craft knife without ruining the surface. They are also marked in 1" (25mm) increments to make lining things up much easier. Some have a metal core and come with magnetic rulers so that you can place your paper on the lines, align the ruler, and have less chance of paper slippage when you make the cut.

Cutting mats come in a variety of sizes, from 4" (102mm) squares for tiny projects to large mats that will cover your entire work surface. The larger mats are available at fabric or discount stores.

Workshop & Kitchen Tools

Many items used in crafting had their beginnings in a kitchen or wood shop.

- Hammers are wonderful for distressing metal objects and adding metal stamps to tags. Some have interchangeable heads with different textures.

- Wire cutters and needle-nosed pliers are a necessity for adding jewelry materials to your work, and it doesn't hurt to have several sizes of the pliers.

- There are tools on the market, found in the model-building section of craft store chains, that can create perfect mitered corners in lightweight wood, paper, and mat board. You can also find sanding blocks there that never wear out as long as you clean them well after each use.

- From your kitchen, grab a handful of wooden skewers to keep near your workspace. They are handy for holding tiny elements in place while the glue dries, even spacing between the spine and covers when making books, and holding tiny bits of low-tack adhesive when placing rhinestones and beads.

- Wax paper and cling wrap can be wadded up and used as a rubber stamp for background effects, and freezer paper can be used to support fabric for printing on your home printer.

Household tools. Many tools used for the projects in this book were easy to find in the kitchen or workshop.

Professional results. Using the proper cutting implements makes all the difference when you want crisp, clean edges on papers, photos, and trims.

Trimmers, Scissors & Knives

Some things you can't live without are the implements for cutting your materials, whether it's paper, cloth, cork, or anything else you believe your project needs. Even if you use a lot of torn edges in your work, you need something to square things up. After that, you can alter the edges any way you like.

TRIMMERS

Paper trimmers range in size from a 12" (305mm) cut up to 3 or 4 feet (915 or 1220mm). Of course, you probably don't need one that big, but when purchasing a new trimmer, first look at your needs.

If you plan to trim nothing larger than a 12" x 12" (305 x 305mm) sheet of scrapbook paper, smaller paper trimmers

are just fine. They have replaceable blades and often come with a scoring blade for creating crisp, straight folds. You can also get decorative blades for some of the larger trimmers for creating scalloped, frayed, or patterned edges. Trimmers range in price from less than $20 to more than $50.

Guillotine cutters, similar to those that we grew up with in school, are preferred by a lot of craft artists. The lower-priced models should only be used for cutting one sheet of paper at a time to avoid shifting, although these have improved in the last few years.

High-end rotary blade trimmers are those made for the professional market, such as photographers. These range in size as well, but have one great feature: most of the blades never need replacing and sharpen themselves with each cut you make. They can also take up to five sheets of 20 lb. bond paper or three sheets of lightweight cardstock at a time, which makes prepping for a class or making 100 Christmas cards less time consuming. They range in price from less than $150 to more than $500. The money you save in replacing blades over a two-year period could pay for the low-to-mid-priced trimmer in no time if you do a lot of cutting.

SCISSORS AND KNIVES

Scissors can be used on fabric or paper, but rarely both, because if you cut paper repeatedly with your fabric scissors, they won't cut cloth (and vice versa). Some scissors make decorative edges and others keep the sticky residue from your last project from transferring to the next one or, worse, building up on the blades so they stick to everything, including themselves. You can also find magnetic scissors, which I thought was a waste at first, then realized they come in handy for picking up tiny metal embellishments for placement on projects.

My recommendation is that you have the following scissors and knives:

Large scissors with titanium blades: These are close to indestructible. I have cut everything from paper to light-gauge wire to thin metal sheeting with mine. The long blades make it easier and quicker to get a straight cut.

Small scissors for getting into tight places: I like the titanium blades for small scissors as well. You never know when you'll need to clip off a tiny piece of metal in a tight corner, and these will handle the job.

Craft knives: These are a staple in the studio. You can cut just about anything with them, including acrylic sheets up to ½" (13mm) thick. Craft knives make trimming excess material a breeze and can also be used for carving. There are the standard models, which are approximately 6" (152mm) long and have easily replaceable blades, and smaller ones that make repeated cuts, such as trimming wood or acrylic, easier on your hands. There are also knives with swivel blades for cutting circles and shapes.

I usually keep two or three knives handy. I use an inexpensive metal-handled one that I bought at the dollar store for paper cutting and trimming the little excess pieces that sometimes appear on die cuts. I also have a couple of nice cushioned-handled knives that I use for cutting things that require repeated strokes. If you plan to cut mat board, for instance, your fingers will appreciate the cushioned grip.

One note of caution: Be very careful with these knives. Always keep them capped when not in use and never use these for a quick cut without paying attention. If you're cutting a thick surface, such as acrylic, don't skimp on the number of strokes it takes to make a good cut. I have sliced across three fingers of my left hand cutting something as lightweight as foam core board, gripping the knife in my right hand, holding the straight-edge with my left, and pushing down to get it all in one cut. It was not a pretty sight and required a trip to the doctor and a tetanus shot.

Terrific tips

If your knife didn't come with a protective cap or you have lost it, the plastic cap from an inexpensive ballpoint pen will work just fine.

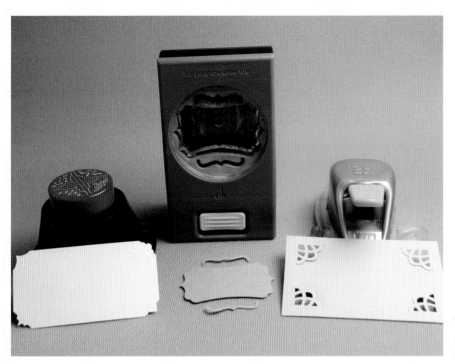

Variety of uses. Hand punches cut everything from delicate corners to layered tags. Some even emboss as they cut.

Punches

What would we do without punches? You can find anything you need from a simple standard hole-punch to punches that handle several separate layers at one time to create a multi-surface embellishment. There are also punches made to punch two different sizes of holes, set large and small eyelets, and punch through several layers of cardstock, chipboard, or thin metal.

HAND-HELD PUNCHES

These are just what they say. You use hand power to make the cuts, so you are a little limited in the thickness of the paper or board you want to cut. If you're punching paper or cardstock, you will be fine. You can get shapes, borders, or alphabet punches. More information is listed under *Die Cuts* in Chapter 2.

HAND-CRANK AND ELECTRIC PUNCHES

These are the big boys. You can cut paper, cardstock, or even multiple layers of both. There are large dies on the market along with specialty dies that cut paper and even mat board and foam sheets into 3-D objects, such as pockets, boxes, or little books. Some punches and die-cutting machines also have embossing capabilities.

CIRCLE CUTTERS

For a long time, my circle cutter was a saucer from my kitchen. I never felt the need for a tool made especially for cutting a circle until I used one. I was hooked. You can cut up to a 6" (152 mm) diameter circle quickly and easily, which means I no longer spend time trying to adjust the circumference of my saucer and can get on to more creative endeavors. The same company also makes a large, round-cornered, rectangle cutter, very useful for adding a large, layered element to a page.

Perfect circles. A circle cutter makes it easy to cut out holes around the handles of the *Can Full of Memories* (p. 64) project.

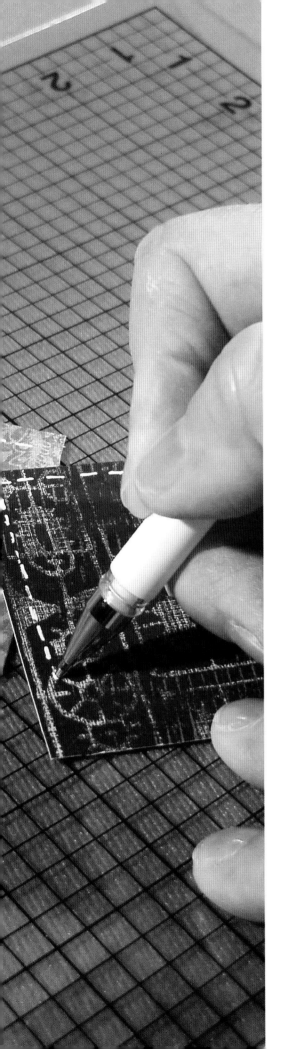

Chapter 2
Techniques

After gathering the necessary tools, it's time to try them out and take your creativity to the next level. Techniques shown in this chapter allow common household items, and others not typically identified with scrapbooking, to be repurposed into extraordinary tribute pieces. From embossing to die cutting and texturizing, it's all in the details.

Adding interest. Layering adds interest, dimension, and a look of sophistication to any project.

Layering

Layering is an easy technique that can multiply the designer look in any project. You simply add another layer or two of cardstock or patterned paper to your base image, such as a photo or tag. It doesn't take much and you don't need a really wide margin per layer—just ⅛" (3mm) to ¼" (6mm) will do just fine.

For a ¼" (6mm) border, measure the base image and add ½" (13mm) to the measurement length and width.

Example: If the photo is 3" x 5" (76 x 127mm), cut the next layer 3½" x 5½" (89 x 140mm). If you want a third layer, add an additional ½" (13mm) to each measurement.

Journaling

Journaling helps to tell the story and ties visual items together. Most often, it takes the form of computer-generated text printed on cardstock but can also come from pages of books or other printed materials.

Pieces can be sponged with ink to add age or framed within bezels as in the *Family Tribute Shelf* (p. 54). Quotes, such as the ones used on the second *Jewelry Box Storage Caddy* (p. 68) or the *Shadow Box Book* (p. 90), can be found for nearly any situation.

The *Can Full of Memories* (p. 64) uses journaling on its base and tag to show specifics about a family trip while the *Keepsake Sewing Box* (p. 76), *Heirloom Stationery Box* (p. 72), *Recipe Serving Tray* (p. 82), and *Fabric Photo Wall Hanging* (p. 110) tell of loving family memories.

Hand-written sentiments are the most precious. If the piece is written by a family ancestor, print a copy rather than using the original.

Nameplates

Nameplates are used on nearly every project in this book. They can be made of die-cut letters, such as those in the *Jewelry Box Storage Caddies* (p. 68), *Recipe Serving Tray* (p. 82), or *Shadow Box Book* (p. 90), or fabric headers like the ones used in the *Fabric Photo Wall Hanging* (p. 110). Others are embossed like the layered tag hanging from the *Can Full of Memories* (p. 64) and die-cut aluminum used on the *Keepsake Sewing Box* (p. 76).

Many nameplates are created from die-cut mat board that has been painted and layered with elegant papers or printed or hand-written sentiments as seen in the *Birthday Card Book* (p. 98) and *Relationship Wall Art* (p. 58). Ornate metal frames serve as nameplates in the *Family Tribute Shelf* (p. 54), as well as the *Heirloom Stationery Box* (p. 72) and *Copper Flower Hanger* (p. 104).

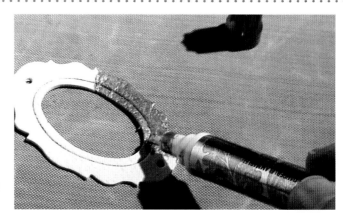

Gold leafing. Gold leaf inking turns a standard die-cut nameplate into a thing of beauty.

Copper. Copper metallic acrylic paint makes an ornate metal nameplate extraordinary.

Terrific tips

To get a good alignment on your title or quotation, cut the die image from clear acetate or a colored paper scrap. Lay the cut-away piece over the quote and lightly trace around it with a pencil. Draw another line ⅛" (3mm) around the outside of the original line and trim on this line. Erase the original line.

When printing your quotes, print more than one and print in various font sizes. You never know when you'll need a second one and it's better to print it and not need it than having to waste another entire sheet of cardstock.

Rubber-Stamping

Basic rubber-stamping is just inking the stamp and applying it to your surface. You can stamp on just about anything that doesn't move too quickly. I have seen stamps on everything from paper to cookies to children. Here are some additional techniques using rubber stamps.

CUSTOMIZING BACKGROUND PAPER

Creating a custom background is easy as pie with rubber stamps, inkpads, and cardstock or paper. Just ink the stamp and apply randomly or in a specific pattern, re-inking between each stamping. Add another stamp design or use the same stamp and coordinating ink for a two-color background.

With patterned papers, inks should be dark or bright enough to stand out. Having a shade of ink slightly darker than your patterned paper will appear subtle and one that is much darker or brighter will give a bold look. Experiment with scrap papers, patterns, and different colors and save them as a reference guide.

Custom background. Plain cardstock becomes custom background paper when stamped. Continue to add additional stamps and ink colors as desired.

Stamping. Add interest by stamping over a printed paper. The combination of the print and your stamped image creates custom paper.

Stamping off

If you want a light blue image and the only ink you have is dark blue, what do you do? Just ink your stamp as usual then stamp it off once or twice on a piece of scrap paper. Huff your breath on the stamp and then apply it to your surface.

When you huff on the stamp, it adds just enough moisture from your breath to keep the ink useable. The result is a light image. You can then stamp another image over it with dark ink. Sometimes, even your scrap paper becomes a beautiful background.

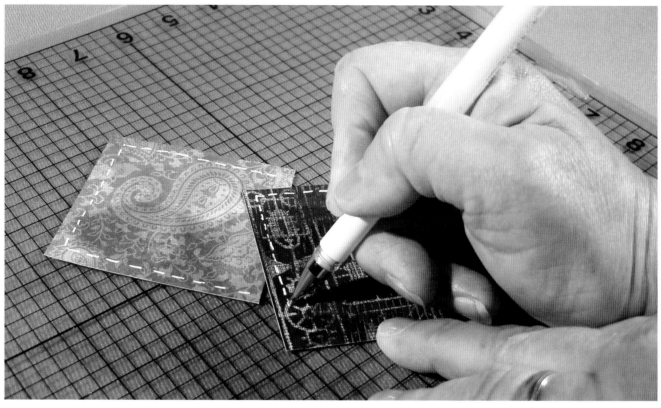

Faux Stitching

If you love the look of stitching on paper, but hate dragging out your sewing machine, these faux stitching techniques are for you.

Just use a white pen to draw tiny dashes in a somewhat straight line to imitate hand stitching. Advanced faux stitching takes a little longer to create but the results are stunning.

Mark the stitching line with a ruler and pencil every ¼" (6mm). Place a rolled tea towel or piece of craft foam under your paper and pierce the paper at every mark with a paper piercer or straight pin. Place your ink pen in each hole and draw a line to the next. If you do it slowly, you'll have a perfect stitching line that Isaac Singer would be proud to call his own. If you speed up the drawing process, you'll get a little bit of curve that is very charming. Try both on scrap cardstock to see which you prefer.

Faux stitching. A white pen and tiny lines imitate machine stitching without the hassle. Use a ruler if you prefer precision, otherwise the piece takes on a hand-stitched look.

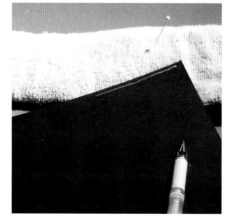

Advanced. Fold a towel as a base beneath your paper. Use a straight pin to punch evenly spaced holes. Draw lines between the holes with a white pen.

Creating leather. The addition of faux stitching makes the embossed cardstock on the *Can Full of Memories* (p. 64) look like a stitched leather luggage tag.

Sponging

Sponging is one easy technique that adds a subtle ton of impact.

There are many types of sponges on the market and all have a use in stamping. My preference is the grout sponge, which can be cut into many pieces. You want to be sure to use a different sponge for each inkpad so that you don't contaminate from one pad to the next.

To give your papers an aged look, press the sponge into a brown inkpad and apply it by using a stroke that is perpendicular to the paper edge. Go all around the edge and the result will be a paper that looks 100 years old.

DIRECT-TO-PAPER INKING

For a distressed look, add a direct-to-paper technique by sliding the inkpad along the edges. This creates irregular streaks along the paper edge. When you are working with very similar colors, this can really help distinguish one layer from the next and add dimension to your project.

Not enough distressed edges? Run the blade of your scissors or use a special tool made for distressing to rough up the edges, then apply the ink again for a great grungy look.

You can use these techniques with layering, applying ink to the original photo or tag as well as successive layers, using the same color or a coordinating color on each layer.

Depth. Sponge edges by inking your sponge on an inkpad. Lightly rub it on the paper edges. It will create the look of acid staining, similar to aged papers, and adds depth.

Inkpad use. Use the edge of your inkpad to rub along the edges of the paper. Don't worry about not having straight ink marks. The dark edges add instant age.

Adding color. Some inkpads can be used as a sponge when applying color directly to paper or cardstock.

Changing color. Originally too bright for the *Relationship Wall Art* project (p. 58), adding ink gave dimension to silk flowers and made them the perfect color.

Textures

Many types of paper available today have texture, from a linen look to layers of heat embossing to flocking. Texture makes your project more interesting when juxtaposed with plain cardstock or additional textures.

There are also many texturing tools on the market, from blind embossing metal plates to heavy-duty embossing machines, so you can create custom paper for projects.

METAL STAMPING

Metal stamping uses a heavy, metal base, a leather pad, metal dies, and a hammer. Many of these items are available at your local hardware store and you can find them all online through merchants who provide jewelry-making supplies.

The stamping technique is particularly beautiful on vintage brass, available in the jewelry-making section of the large chain craft stores. Some independent scrapbook stores carry them as well.

My favorite technique is to pound the metal disk or rectangle to add texture.

The pounding compresses the metal, and you will get edges that aren't perfectly round or square anymore.

When you are satisfied with the edges, use your metal letters or shapes. Place the metal disk or rectangle on the metal base, secure it with masking tape, and strike it hard once or twice with your hammer, being careful not to move the die. Repeat until you are satisfied with the results.

You can use the metal tag as-is or add permanent ink to the impressed design, then sand or wipe off the entire surface.

Terrific tips

Some plain alphabet metal stamps are available at larger hardware stores, but there are also shapes and fancy alphabets made especially for stampers and scrapbookers that you can purchase online. Try to find a shipper who offers free or low-cost shipping. Metal weighs a lot!

Adding texture. Using the metal block as a base, hammer the shape to add texture. Punch letters into the metal with a hammer and die. Hit each letter several times being careful to keep it in place.

Metallic finish. Highlight surfaces with wax metallic finish.

Personalization. Attaching a metal charm to a hammered nametag, such as this one for the *Shadow Box Book* project (p. 90), further personalizes the sentiment.

Accent lettering. Add alcohol ink to make the letters stand out. Make sure it seats in the indentations and wipe off any excess. Permanent marker also works well.

MECHANICAL EMBOSSING

The procedure is the same for most machines. Just place your cardstock in the embossing folder, sandwich it between the proper plates, and crank the handle to run it through the machine. The result is a beautiful, textured piece of cardstock or metal.

There are many texturing plates available for these machines. Most are limited to 6" (152mm) widths and up to 24" (610mm) depths.

EMBOSSING TEMPLATES

There are many templates available that are made from a dense polymer material and require several tools to create your designs. They are made to work with thin metal sheets, which are available in the base metal colors but also come in beautiful blues, greens, and reds. You can use these templates with a Sizzix Big Shot machine with beautiful results. One of the advantages of embossing templates is they are larger than embossing folders, so you can cover a larger surface.

If you do not have a mechanical embossing machine, you can lay metal on top of the template, rub the entire surface with a paper stump, then trace around the shapes to bring out the details. Work on one side, then flip the metal sheet over and work on the other side for some unique effects.

Textures. Place cardstock in an embossing folder and insert it into the embossing machine to texturize. If necessary, the cardstock can be moved so that the entire area can be embossed.

Study first. Hand-crank machines take the work out of embossing and die cutting. Before purchasing a machine, familiarize yourself with each brand's attributes. All do a great job and some will accept other manufacturers' dies and embossing plates.

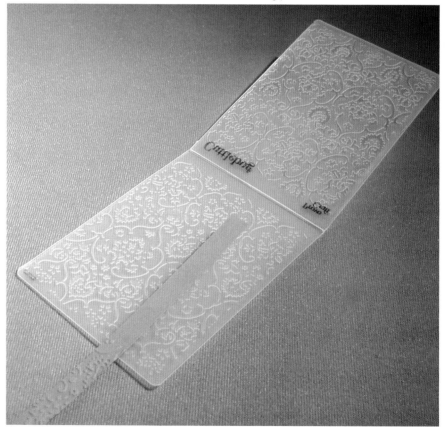

Texturizing. Templates add texture when used with a Sizzix Big Shot embossing and die-cutting machine.

SIMPLE BLIND EMBOSSING

If you don't have the equipment for mechanical embossing, blind embossing gives a tone-on-tone effect, which is beautiful for simple, elegant tags or card fronts.

You will need a light box, available at your craft store, a metal stylus, and a metal embossing plate, which looks much like a metal stencil. Tape the metal plate to the light surface and position your cardstock over it. Tape the cardstock to secure. When the light is turned on, you can see the image. Use the stylus to press along the lines of the metal plate. Once you have your image embossed, you can use it as-is or lightly brush over the raised surface with ink, paint, or chalk.

Aluminum. Colored aluminum sheets can be easily embossed with texture plates, like the nameplates created for the *Keepsake Sewing Box* (p. 76).

RUTH SKINNER WINDHAM
Master Seamstress

Terrific tips

If you don't have a light box available, tape the metal plate and cardstock on the glass of a sunny window for the same effect. Of course, this limits your embossing time to daylight hours.

Die Cuts

Several machines on the market today both emboss and die cut depending on the plate you insert into the machine. Most involve several plates of various depths, an embossing folder, and a hand-crank. There are also some electric machines on the market that make embossing much easier. Some even allow you to create original designs on your computer for embossing, die cutting, or drawing.

Die cut machines have made customizing a project so much simpler. There are dies for cutting paper, cardstock, and even mat board. You can cut anything from simple shapes for embellishments to 3-D objects such as miniature houses and boxes.

Sandwiched. When die cutting with a Big Shot, the die and paper, fabric, or metal, are layered between two cutting pads before moving through the machine.

Dual capability. The Sizzix Big Shot die cuts and embosses.

Metal options. Even thin metals can be cut and texturized. Die cut metal shapes, emboss, and then add more color variety with alcohol inks (p. 26).

Layering swirls. Die-cut swirls can be layered on top of cardstock, or tucked underneath for more interest as with *Relationship Wall Art* (p. 58). Use the same swirl design repeatedly without it looking the same, particularly when cutting papers that have different designs on each side.

Polymer Clay

Clay, one of my favorite childhood mediums, has grown up. There are baked clays, air-dry clays, and even liquid polymer clays. Polymer clay is used for making jewelry and three-dimensional objects and can even be used to cover wooden, papier-mâché, or metal containers or shapes.

Polymer clay is perfect for creating custom embellishments. You can design your own shapes or use plastic molds made especially for this medium. Clay can be painted, sanded, or distressed for wonderful pieces to add to your projects.

Clay prep. Soften clay by massaging it in your hands or running through a pasta machine several times, then roll it out on a non-stick surface. Caution: Never use the pasta machine for anything but polymer once you have taken that route.

Texturing clay. Press a texture plate over the rolled clay. You can purchase texturing tools, but look around the house for common items such as paper clips, cording, keys, etc. Use a cookie cutter or clay cutter to cut out the button shape.

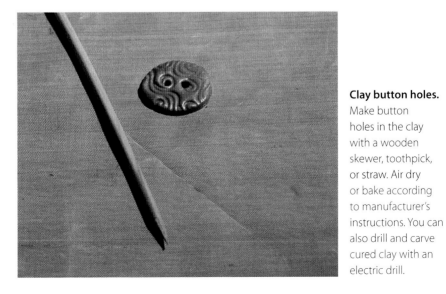

Clay button holes. Make button holes in the clay with a wooden skewer, toothpick, or straw. Air dry or bake according to manufacturer's instructions. You can also drill and carve cured clay with an electric drill.

Eyelets

Eyelets were originally used for reinforcing holes in fabric or leather. Today, we use them for the same thing, but add them to paper as well. Not only are they perfect for adding wire or ribbon to a project, but they can also be used to create shapes and come in several sizes and colors.

Setting an eyelet is simple. The first method is to punch the desired size hole with a punch. Insert your eyelet and lay the eyelet and paper face down on your surface. Place the eyelet setter in the hole of the eyelet and hit the top of the shaft several times with your hammer. If there are any small pieces of metal showing when you remove the setter, just tap it with your hammer to flatten.

You can also purchase a machine that can punch holes and set eyelets, making setting eyelets easy for even the most arthritic hands.

Punching eyelets. Use your hammer and eyelet hole punch tool to make a hole where you want to set the eyelet. There are also inexpensive machines made to punch the hole and set the eyelet with one motion.

Placing eyelets. Place the eyelet in the hole with the back of the eyelet and the back of the paper facing up.

Setting eyelets. Place the eyelet setter in the eyelet hole and hammer to flatten.

Resin

Resins have been on the market for several years, but the latest ones are much easier to use than previous materials. They are made by mixing two ingredients together in equal parts.

You can create jewelry, beautiful papers, or custom embellishments with resins. You still have to wait for them to set up, which can be overnight to several days, depending on the thickness.

For creating jewelry or an embellishment piece using a metal bezel, simply cut out an image, such as a photo printed on your home printer, adhere it securely in the bezel, allow it to dry completely, then fill it with resin. The newer resins dome naturally without air bubbles. If you do experience bubbles, just use a small needle or straight pin to guide them to the edge of the piece for removal. Allow the piece to set according to the manufacturer's directions.

Resin. Resins come in pre-measured dispensers. Combine according to the manfacturer's directions and fill a bezel covering the photo or journaling.

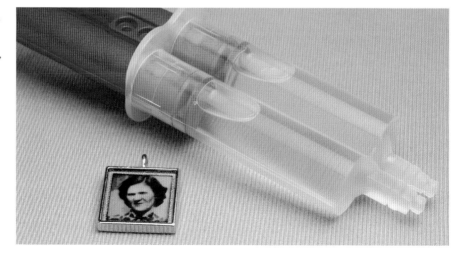

Basic Heat Embossing

I fell in love with rubber-stamping one Saturday morning while visiting with friends in their stamp-making business. When I saw what could be done with embossing powders, I was hooked.

Embossing powders come in every color of the rainbow and in several weights. The primary use is on paper, but they can also be used to fill collage art in bezels or for making embellishments.

Stamp an image with a similar shade of pigment ink or clear embossing ink. Pour embossing powder over the stamped area, and tap off the excess, into a tray made for this purpose or onto a sheet of scrap paper, to return it to its container. Tap the back of the paper to remove any stray bits of embossing powder. You can also use colored embossing powder and stamp the image with a pigment ink or clear embossing ink.

Apply your heat tool to raise and set the image. Gently heat the area, keeping the tool about six inches from the paper and moving the tool so that you don't remain in the same place too long. You can burn your paper, which in some cases might be desirable for a distressed look, but not generally acceptable. You will see when the powder begins to melt. There will be a point when the powder looks a little like orange peel and you think it is finished, but keep heating until you have a nice, smooth surface.

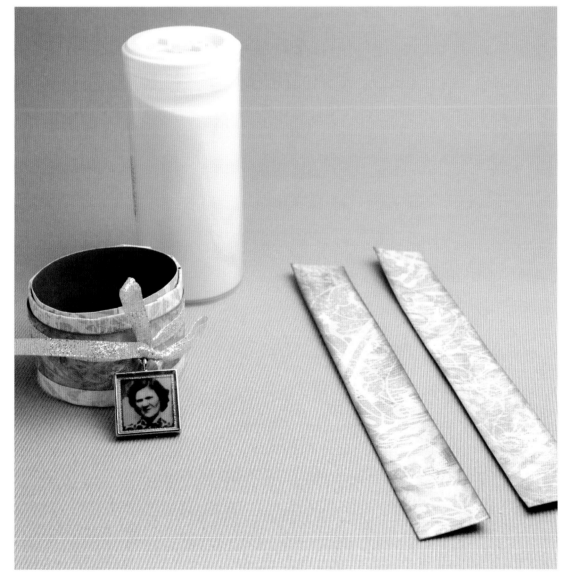

Options on paper. Prepare paper by adding ink, stamping images, and sponging edges for color.

Embossing powder. Stamp the image to be embossed using clear embossing ink or pigment ink in a matching color. Pour embossing powder over the area stamped. Catch the overflow. Tap paper to remove excess powder. Return excess embossing powder to its original container.

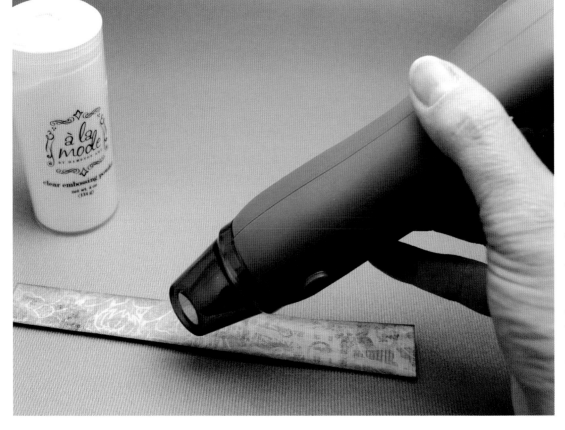

Apply heat. Use a heat tool to melt embossing powder, raising and setting the embossed image. Keep the heat tool moving to prevent burning. When the powder has the appearance of cottage cheese, it's almost ready. Heat a little longer for a nice, smooth finish.

Raised area. The stamped area created by heat embossing is raised and reflective. The strip in the foreground shows embossing powder before it was heated.

Terrific tips

To minimize stray bits of embossing powder sticking to your piece, dust an anti-static product especially made for embossing over the surface before stamping. There will be a small amount of powder residue left on your paper, but it is easily removed with a microfiber towel or dusting sheet.

Eliminate static. Apply anti-static pouch to the inked paper to avoid stray embossing powder flakes.

Batik Embossing

I don't know if batik is the proper term for this embossing technique, but the results are the same no matter what it's called. You can use clear ink and emboss with clear embossing powder for a dynamic look.

Stamp the image and use a heat tool as with basic heat embossing (p. 47). Then use a sponge (p. 39) or the direct-to-paper ink technique (p. 39) to change the color of your paper. When you have added as much ink in as many colors as you like, wipe the entire surface with a paper towel. The embossing will protect the original colors, making the design of your stamp really stand out.

Emboss images. Stamp your image with clear or pigment ink, add embossing powder, and heat with an embossing tool to melt (p. 48).

Add ink in layers. Add colors as desired using the sponging (p. 39) or direct-to-paper (p. 39) methods of application.

Color saturation. Make sure the final layer is very saturated with color. You will still be able to see the original pattern, which gives your piece a more intricate appearance.

Excess ink. Wipe the image with a paper towel to remove any ink remaining on the embossed areas. With clear embossing, the paper's original color shows through. This technique is beautiful for background images.

Tying It Up

Ribbons, string, raffia, cording, and embroidery floss—all make great embellishments for your work. Just tie them on or thread them through a punched hole for instant appeal. They can be tied with a bow, simple knots, or fancy knots.

The Lark's Head Knot is one of the most popular knots used in crafting because it is easy-to-make and beautiful as well.

Insert loop. Fold the ribbon in half and insert the loop through the tag hole, back to front.

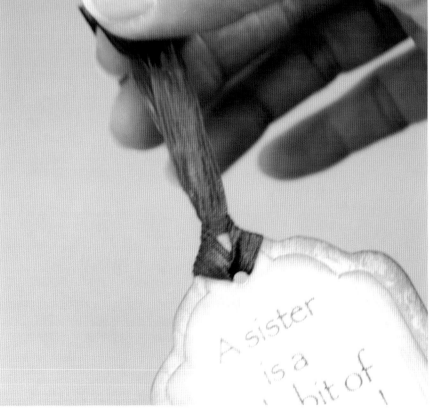

Form a knot. Bring the loop up from the front and insert the ribbon ends into the loop. Pull taut to form the knot. If you are using a slippery ribbon, such as silk or embroidery threads, add a tiny drop of glue to hold it in place. You can also insert the loop from the back for a totally different look.

Chapter 3
On-the-Wall Projects

Put your memories in plain sight. Using the techniques you have learned, favorite family photos become a lasting tribute when displayed on a multi-tiered wooden shelf (p. 54) or behind glass (p. 58). Projects can be easily adapted to any subject matter or decorating style.

MOTHERS & DAUGHTERS

Family Man

athlete (ath'lete) n. 1 competitor in sports; one trained in great physical skill and strength.

- Played on Mississippi State Champion High School Basketball Team
- Fought in Golden Gloves Boxing in the '40s

comedian (ko me' di an) n. An actor in a comedy or a writer of comedies; a comical person.

- He always kept us laughing

father (fä' thur) n.1. A male parent. 2. (F-) God; fathers, ancestors.

- Father of Candice Lee Cofer and Mary Lynn Cofer

husband (huz' band) n. 1. A man who has a wife. 2. A farmer.

- Born on a farm in Water Valley, Mississippi in 1928
- Husband of Elsie Lucille Wilson for more than 30 years.

patriot (pa' tre ut) n. One who is devoted to his country.

- Served in the Army as an M.P. during WWII. Stationed in the Phillipines

pressman (pres'man) n. One who operates or works about a printing press.

- He was an excellent pressman and printed one of Elvis Presley's first record covers.

JACK

Allie Goforth Cofer

Oyer Jackson Cofer (far right)

Mary Ruth Skinner Windham

Family Tribute Shelf

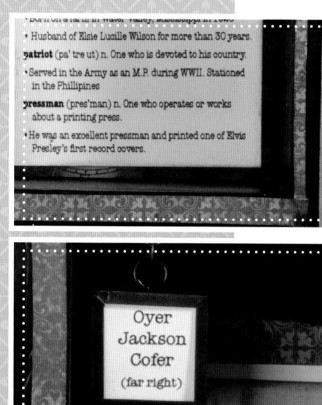

- Born on a farm in Water Valley, Mississippi in 1920
- Husband of Elsie Lucille Wilson for more than 30 years.

patriot (pa' tre ut) n. One who is devoted to his country.

- Served in the Army as an M.P. during WWII. Stationed in the Phillipines

pressman (pres'man) n. One who operates or works about a printing press.

- He was an excellent pressman and printed one of Elvis Presley's first record covers.

Oyer
Jackson
Cofer
(far right)

When the country-decorating craze was so popular, little wooden shelves with cut-out hearts appeared everywhere: gift shops, discount stores—even grocery stores carried them. Today you can find them at your local charity store because people just don't use this style anymore.

My father was a printer. He had black fingernails from manually adding ink to the presses, worked long hours, and always came home with the scent of printing ink in his clothes. That is still one of my favorite scents.

Here's a twist on how I used one of these old shelves, to honor my father's legacy, his work, and his parents, and made the shelf new again.

This project is great for using up odd-sized sheets of scrap cardstock.

Top: Journaling with layered, sponged edges.
Middle: Journaling in metal frames with jump rings serves to identify the individuals in the photos.
Bottom: Ephemera letterpress blocks relate to my father's career.

Ephemera (p. 13)

Coordinating papers (p. 16)

Layered with sponged edges (p. 35)

Journaling in metal frames with jump rings (p. 57)

Coordinating papers (p. 16)

Hardware (p. 24)

Nameplate (p. 36)

Journaling (p. 35)

Layered photo with sponged edges (p. 35)

Sponged cardstock edges (p. 39)

Family Man

JACK

Allie Goforth Cofer

Siblings Mitchell, Earl and Ginger

Oyer Jackson Cofer (far right)

The Family Still

Tools & Supplies

- Multi-layered wooden shelf

- Spray paint: black

- Sandpaper

- Printed cardstock: 12" x 12" (305 x 305mm) for sides and fronts, scraps for photos, assorted coordinating sheets

- Cardstock scraps: cream

- Ink pads: brown and black

- Photos and ephemera of your choice

- Metal scrapbook hardware frames, 1" (25mm) square, four

- Small screw eyes, two

- Chipboard or cardboard cut to fit the back of the shelf (if back is open)

- Chipboard or cardstock scraps for patterns

- Strong, clear-drying adhesive

- Foam board scraps

- Hardware embellishments: knob, nameplate

Techniques

Scrapbooking goes 3-D when combined with a previously retired wooden shelf. Basic layering and sponging add dimension to photos while simple journaling is made elegant when showcased in metal framework. Add some ephemera and hardware and it's a tribute any father would envy.

1. Paint the wooden shelf. Lightly sand the wooden shelf. Don't worry if there are dents or cuts. They just add character. Wipe it down with a damp cloth. Apply two coats of black paint. Allow it to dry between coats.

2. Create patterns for cutting papers. Measure sides of the shelf and cut chipboard patterns ¼" (6mm) smaller all around. To cover the curved space on the front and hide the heart cut-out, place the chipboard on the surface to be covered, trace the curve, and make sure of the fit, trimming as necessary. When you are satisfied with the fit of all patterns, trace on printed paper, cut, and adhere to the shelf. If your shelf side is longer than 12" (305mm), you will need to match paper patterns to achieve the necessary length.

Terrific tips

If the match line between papers is very visible, you can cover it by inking a background or swirl stamp (p. 39) and stamping the entire side. This also adds more interest to your project.

Allie Goforth Cofer

Siblings Mitchell, Earl and Ginger

Oyer Jackson Cofer (far right)

The Family Still

detail

3. Covering the shelf back. If your shelf has an open back, measure the openings and cut printed cardstock ¼" (6mm) larger all around. Lay the shelf on chipboard or cardboard and mark openings. Adhere papers to the chipboard to cover each background opening, then adhere the chipboard to the back of the shelf with the papers showing through the openings. Cut ¼" (6mm) printed cardstock and adhere to shelf fronts. Cut additional pieces to cover any exposed areas.

4. Add photos and journaling. Print photos, titles, and journaling and either trim out with ⅛" (3mm) of white space showing around each edge or layer them on cream cardstock and trim (p. 35). Cover foam board scraps with printed cardstock and trim to ½" (13mm) larger all around than your photos and journaling blocks. Sponge all edges with brown ink (p. 39), then adhere layers. Glue additional foam board scraps to the back of the pieces for dimension, bringing them forward on the shelves. Adhere stacked photos to the shelf background.

5. Attach hanging metal frames. Place small journaling inside metal frames. Add jump rings to connect the frames and beads, if desired. Insert tiny screw eyes into the underside of the shelf above the photo and attach the frames with a jump ring.

6. Attach ephemera and hardware. Adhere any ephemera to the shelves. Because my father was printer, I chose to add his name in letterpress blocks, available at antique stores, to the top shelf. Add additional hardware, such as the drawer pull on the bottom shelf or the metal frame nameplate at the top.

Terrific tips

- Purchase small frames inexpensively at a dollar store and use them in place of the foam board mounts. They can be adhered in place, or you can leave them unattached so that you can change out the photos occasionally.

- If you can't find colored screw eyes, color them with alcohol ink (p. 26) or a permanent marker to blend in with the background.

Chapter 3 • On-the-Wall Projects • Family Tribute Shelf

Relationship Wall Art

There is a special bond between mothers and daughters and grandmothers and granddaughters that is like no other. Our mothers and grandmothers know exactly what we are going through at every milestone in our lives: the excitement and uncertainty of the first day of school, our nervousness during first dates, the anxiety over our school grades, and the fun of sleepovers with our girlfriends. They know how we feel when we've found the right man to spend the rest of our lives with, and the joy that comes with the birth of a child. They are there to laugh and cry with us and sometimes set us straight when we've gotten off the straight and narrow path.

This project celebrates the kinship between these women who are my husband's sister, mother, and grandmother. They have a fortitude that comes with meeting life head-on, always seeing the glass half-full, and doing their best no matter what.

This versatile design will make wonderful wall art for fathers and sons, sisters and brothers, best friends, or pets. It would also be the perfect Sweet Sixteen birthday gift, with baby photos, gangly little girl pictures, and a poised, young-woman portrait. The sky's the limit!

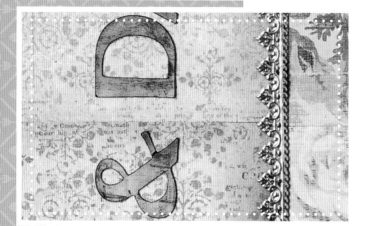

Top: A die-cut nameplate and a margin of colored paper around each photo add nice touches.
Middle: Die-cut swirls and faux flowers.
Bottom: Die-cut letters and coordinating papers.

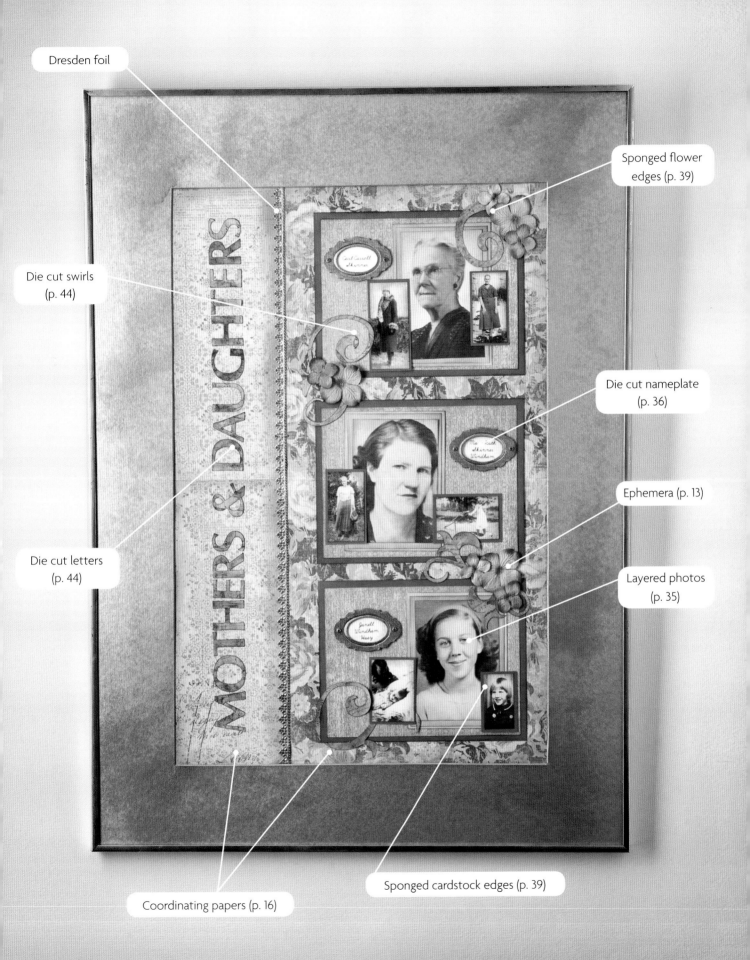

Dresden foil

Sponged flower edges (p. 39)

Die cut swirls (p. 44)

Die cut nameplate (p. 36)

Ephemera (p. 13)

Die cut letters (p. 44)

Layered photos (p. 35)

Sponged cardstock edges (p. 39)

Coordinating papers (p. 16)

MOTHERS & DAUGHTERS

Tools & Supplies

- Mat board: 16" x 24" (406 x 610mm)

- Mat board scraps

- Printed cardstock: 12" x 12" (305 x 305mm), two sheets of one floral pattern/color, one coordinating pattern/color (left column), and three of a double-sided paper or cardstock in an additional pattern/color (for photo blocks, swirls, and title)

- Solid color cardstock: 8½" x 11" (215 x 280mm), three sheets olive green, two sheets cream, and two sheets light green

- Die-cutting machine

- Swirl and nameplate dies

- Paper or silk flowers

- Gold leafing pen or gold spray paint

- Dresden foil border: 24" (610mm)

- Adhesive

- Computer-generated names and photos

- Chalk inks: brown, light pink, and olive

- Small brads: six

Techniques

Elegance abounds. Simple sponging, layered photos, and die-cut lettering and swirls, combined with beautiful papers and Dresden foil, provide a fitting background for three generations of matriarchs. Die-cut nameplates are painted gold. Even the silk flowers are sponged.

1. Cover the background. Cut a single sheet of printed cardstock to two 6" x 12" (152 x 305mm) sheets. Sponge long edges with brown ink (p. 39). Adhere them to the left side of the mat board, one above the other, to cover the background. Use two coordinating sheets of cardstock to cover the right side. Adhere Dresden foil border to cover the vertical paper seam.

2. Layer photos. Trim olive cardstock to 8½" x 6½" (216 x 165mm) and sponge edges with brown ink. Adhere on floral background 1½" (38mm) from top edge and ¾" (19mm) between olive sheets, centering on floral paper from left to right.

Cut two sheets of remaining printed paper to three blocks, 8" x 6" (203 x 152mm). Sponge edges and adhere to olive blocks, leaving a ¼" (6mm) edge all around.

Mount small photos on olive cardstock scraps. Mount large photos on light green and cream cardstock, being sure to sponge all edges with brown ink before adhering. Adhere to printed paper/olive blocks according to photo.

detail

Terrific tips

Purchased nameplates cut from metal or chipboard also work well.

For a handmade touch, use an acid-free journaling pen to write the names. Your descendants will be happy to see your own handwriting and make this future heirloom more valuable to them!

3. Assemble nameplates. Cut nameplates with die-cutting machine and paint with gold leafing pen or spray paint. Print names on cream cardstock, trim, and adhere to the back of the frames so that they are centered when viewed from the front. Add brads and secure to each photo block with strong, clear-drying adhesive.

4. Die cut letters and swirls. Die cut swirls from green cardstock and title letters from the reverse side of the paper used for the photo blocks. Ink all edges and sponge all three inks randomly on the surfaces. Ink flowers in the same manner. Adhere swirls over and under cardstock photo blocks for added interest. Attach flowers. Adhere lettering, centering on the left-side.

Chapter 4
Dual-Purpose Storage Projects

These storage pieces tell a story and are functional as well as decorative. Turn a paint can into a protector of larger memories (p. 64), convert jewelry boxes into storage caddies (p. 68), transform a cigar box into an heirloom (p. 72), and create a lovely sewing box from a paper maché blank (p. 76).

Can Full of Memories

My family loves to travel, and I am always on the lookout for little remembrances of our trips, whether they are dried flowers pressed in a book, little containers of dirt or sand, pretty pebbles, or purchased items from a gift shop.

In 2005, we took a driving mega-trip, which involved traveling more than 9,000 miles and visiting 14 national parks and 17 states. Every time we stopped at someplace special, I would find something by which to remember it. I also picked up lots of brochures in the welcome centers, which were great for inclusion in my trip scrapbook, but what was I going to do with all those multi-dimensional objects?

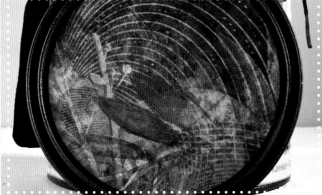

My solution? A container with a lid that I could place on a bookshelf, an end or bedside table, or a desktop. This container houses most of my precious mementos from the trip, and I always know where they are without having to dig through closets when I want to reminisce. The colors work well with my home décor, so I am very proud to display these in any room.

This project also makes a wonderful gift for a new mother in which to keep all of her baby's firsts: socks and shoes, bibs, teething ring, spoon, cup, etc.

Top: Layered photos highlight vacation destinations.
Middle: Metallic paint over paper.
Bottom: Textured cardstock tag with journaling and ephemera embellishment.

Metallic paint (p. 27)

Coordinating papers (p. 16)

Leather

Layered photos (p. 35)

Eyelet (p. 46)

Journaling (p. 35)

Ephemera (p. 13)

Layered tag (p. 35)

Sponged edges (p. 39)

Embossing (p. 42)

Faux stitching (p. 38)

Journaling (p. 35)

Supplies

- Paint can with lid, one-gallon size

- Printed cardstock: 12" x 12" (305 x 305mm), two identical sheets and one coordinating sheet

- Solid cardstock: 8½" x 11" (216 x 279mm), two sheets or enough coordinating scraps to mount all photos

- Cardstock: 8½" x 11" (216 x 279mm), one each, rust and cream

- Cardstock: 4¼" x 2½" (108 x 64mm), two pieces, dark brown

- Photos: 3" x 2" (76 x 51mm) for this sample, approximately 12

- Leather strips: 1 yard (915mm) each, three coordinating colors

- Ball chain and clasp: 7" (178mm), black

- Metal embellishments: charms, pins, or pressed pennies

- Circle punch: 1" (25mm)

- Spray paint: dark brown

- Adhesive

- Rubber bands

- Self-sealing plastic wrap (optional)

- Flexible tape measure

- Chalk ink: rust and dark brown

- Large eyelet: copper

- Eyelet-setting equipment

- Circle cutter: 6" (152mm), or round object to use as a pattern

Techniques

Transform a paint can with coordinating papers, layered photos, and ephemera of choice. Then personalize with journaling, shading for interest. Add an embossed, layered nameplate tag with faux stitching and sponging and it looks like leather!

Terrific tips

Vertical stripes work particularly well for the sides of the can because they are easy to match at the seams.

1. Paint the can. Wipe the paint can to remove dust and apply two coats of brown spray paint, inside and out. Allow it to dry.

2. Trim printed cardstock to fit over the handles. Using a tape measure, determine the distance between the centers of the handle and the distance from the top of the can to the center of the handle. Line up the 1" (25mm) punch so that the edge of the paper is slightly inside the punch area and the circle is open on the edge. Cut the holes that will go around the handles. Sponge top and bottom edges and adhere both sheets to the can, overlapping at the handles.

3. Prepare photos. Trim photos and adhere to rust cardstock, leaving a ⅛" (3mm) border all around (p. 35). Mount layered photos to the can with quick-drying adhesive. This can be tricky because of the curve of the can surface, but once you have them all arranged, slip on as many rubber bands as necessary to hold the photos in place, lining them up over all the corners and as many of the sides as possible. In addition to the rubber bands, you can also wrap the can with self-sealing plastic wrap, drawing it tightly to keep the photo edges pressed in place. Allow the glue to dry.

4. Add journaling. Print your journaling on cream cardstock. (I used the names of all the states we visited.) Trim to the can's circumference and ½" (13mm) tall. Sponge edges and adhere to the lower edge of the can.

5. Embellish the can. Cut a 6" (152mm) circle from coordinating printed cardstock and adhere it to the lid. If desired, use metallic paints to accent patterns on the lid and sides (p. 27). Braid three leather strips. Tie to one side of paint can handle. Wrap around the paint can handle and tie securely to the other side. Allow ends to hang loosely.

6. Create the tag. To make the tag, cut two pieces of dark brown cardstock to 4¼" x 2½" (108 x 64mm) and add texture with texture plate (p. 42). Cut a window from one tag piece, 2¾" x 1½" (70 x 38mm). Add faux stitching (p. 38) with a white pen around the cutout and around edges, front and back. Print the trip information label on cream cardstock, gently sponge with rust ink (p. 39), and center it in the brown tag opening. Adhere both sides together and trim corners with a corner rounder punch. Add an eyelet (p. 46) and string onto the ball chain. Attach the tag and any additional embellishments to the paint can handle.

Jewelry Box Storage Caddies

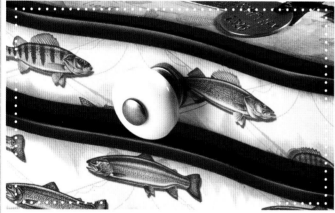

With the paperless technology available to us today, we don't always need the everyday items we have been accustomed to having in our office areas: pencils, pens, paper clips, notepads, etc. It's all right there on our computer. Need to attach papers together? Create a new folder. Make notes? Pull up a digital notepad. Write notes in the margin? Word documents have that advantage built in.

One of the joys of having my own home office is that I love a pretty, yet functional, work area, and, I must confess, I have a love affair with tactile office supplies, second only to my love of hardware stores. I was a paper collector long before the term came into use as a person who buys pretty printed papers for scrapbooking, only to hoard them away and pull them out like a miser with his gold.

All that being said, I still like an uncluttered desk space, so I've created this little Office-in-a-Box, one for me and one for my husband who shares the office with me. They have everything we need and also incorporate recycled jewelry boxes, a fact that makes my heart feel very green!

Top: Die-cut nameplate with fishing fly embellishment.
Middle: Cardstock-covered drawer with hardware drawer pull.
Bottom: Photo with sponged edges layered with embossed cardstock.

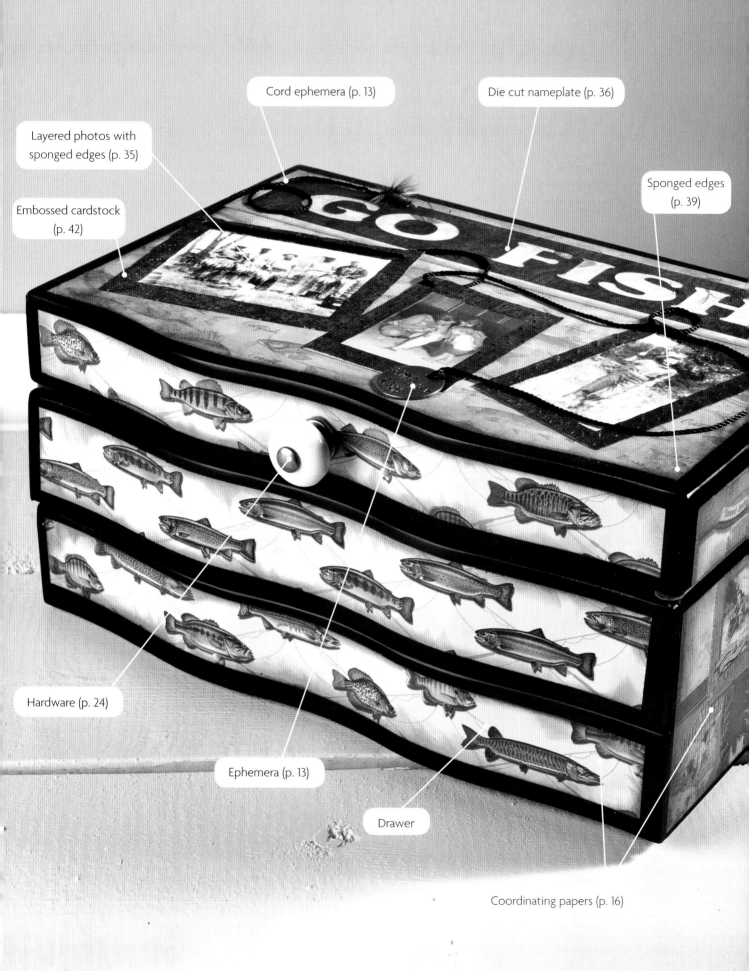

Layered photos with sponged edges (p. 35)

Cord ephemera (p. 13)

Die cut nameplate (p. 36)

Sponged edges (p. 39)

Embossed cardstock (p. 42)

Hardware (p. 24)

Ephemera (p. 13)

Drawer

Coordinating papers (p. 16)

Tools & Supplies

- Recycled wooden jewelry box

- Printed cardstock: 12" x 12" (305 x 305mm), four coordinating sheets

- Solid cardstock to match printed cardstock: 8½" x 11" (216 x 279mm), one sheet

- Coordinating ink

- Metal embellishments

- Strong white glue

- Sandpaper

- Drawer pull

- Fishing-themed photos

- Fishing fly

- Nylon woven fishing line: 18" (457mm)

Techniques

Coordinating papers enter the third dimension, covering the lids, sides, and drawer fronts of these jewelry boxes. Personalization is easy with layered photos, embossed cardstock, sponged edges, and a die-cut nameplate. Finish with ephemera of choice and a glass knob handle.

These directions are for the fishing-themed box, but Box #2 is assembled the same except for the lid embellishments.

1. Prepare the box surface. Lightly sand any rough spots on the box and wipe it down with a damp cloth. Allow it to dry.

2. Paper the lid, sides, and back. Measure top, sides, and back of the box lid. Cut cover papers ¼" (6mm) smaller all around, sponge the edges with coordinating ink (p. 39), and adhere them to the appropriate areas. Do the same for the sides and the back.

3. Add nameplate and photos to the top. Cut *Go Fish* with an electronic cutting machine using the solid cardstock. Reserve the letters for another project and trim the letter outline block to fit on top of the box lid.

4. Apply front papers. Cut a different printed paper into strips ½" (13mm) less than the depth and width of the lid, middle panel, and bottom drawer fronts. If your box measures more than 12" (305mm) wide, you will need to match patterns when adhering papers.

Sponge the edges with coordinating ink, and adhere strips to the appropriate areas keeping ¼" (6mm) of the box showing all around.

5. Add photos and ephemera to the lid. Cut solid cardstock the size of each photo. Add texture with a texture plate (p. 42) and cut a window from each, creating a frame. Adhere frames over the photos. Punch a tiny hole in a corner of each framed photo through which to wind the black cording. Lay cording across the lid, looping through and around photos. Adhere photos and cording in place. Add a fishing fly to one end of the cording and a metal charm to the other. Attach a drawer pull to the lid or drawer front to finish.

Terrific tips

- Immediately after a gift-giving holiday, stores mark down merchandise rather than holding it for a year until the holiday rolls around again. You can find items like these jewelry boxes for a steal.

- Remove lid hinges from the box before attaching papers for a clean finish, then reattach.

Box #2

The second box is for my side of the office. My husband always said that I went to work every day and colored. He's right. I am a graphic designer, fine artist, and mixed media artist, doing what I love every day, so this quote from Confucius pretty well sums up my career: "Find a job that you love and you'll never have to work a day in your life."

I used a flower die to cut the flowers from thin cork. They were then stamped and inked and adhered to the box top in sets of two, except for the smallest flowers. Embellishments included metal brads, a cameo, and resin button for centers (p. 22). On the large flower, I added pop dots under the petals to add interest. The nameplate (p. 36) is also from a die, cut from mat board. I sprayed it with platinum spray paint for a touch of elegance.

Heirloom Stationery Box

My parents, Elsie Lucille Wilson and Jack Cofer, met while working at the Nabisco Factory in Memphis in the '40s. He worked on the mezzanine floor, which overlooked where she worked on the first floor. He threw a cracker at her to get her attention and the rest is history.

He enlisted in the Army and was sent to the Philippines as a military police officer as part of the cleanup process after World War II. My mother was a prolific letter writer and, since mail was slow then, Daddy received mail from home bi-weekly at best. One day, he received not just a few letters, but an entire bag of mail, all from my mother. That was about the same time he got his typical Army tattoo, a heart with her name on his upper arm.

Daddy passed away in 1977 as a result of wounds he received in WWII. My mother remained a letter writer for the rest of her life. She never forgot any birthdays of friends and relatives and all their children and even wrote letters to me, though we both lived in the same city. These will provide material for future projects to honor my mother.

I hope to be the kind of letter-writer she was, warming hearts when they see the handwritten return address.

I wish this box held those love letters she wrote, but they are long since gone. I keep my note cards, favorite pen, and a book of stamps in this altered cigar box right beside my comfy chair so they are always ready and waiting for me to spend the evening writing notes to those I love.

Top: Nameplate with journaling.
Middle: Layered photo and journaling with sponged edges.
Bottom: Hardware corner pieces.

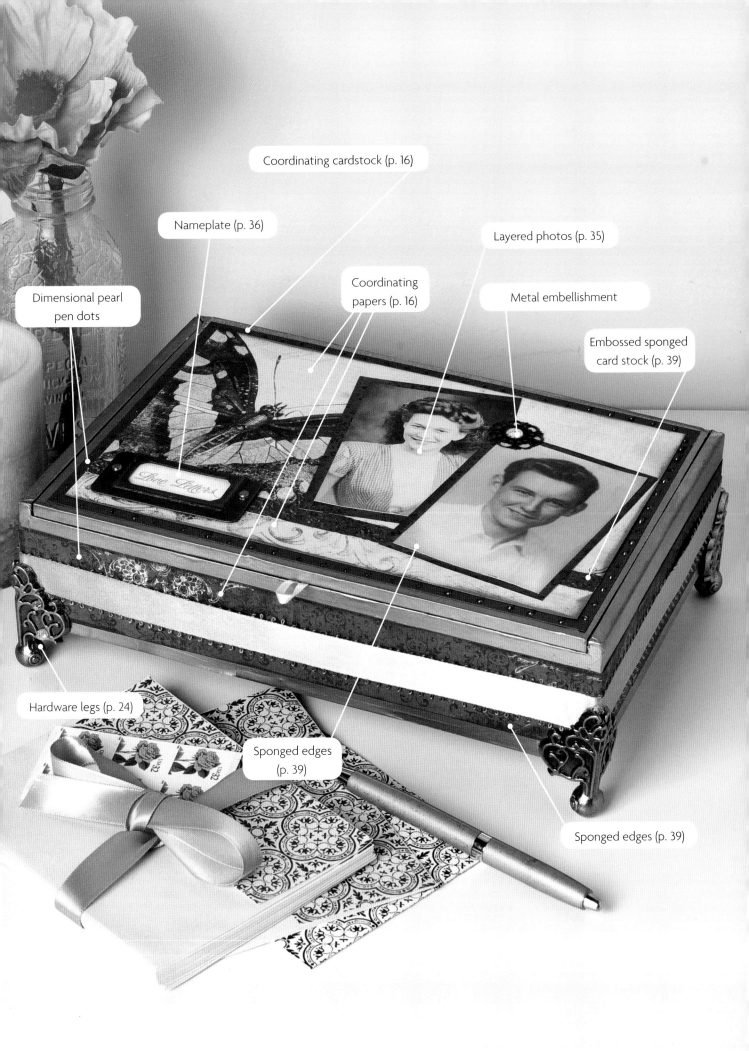

Coordinating cardstock (p. 16)

Nameplate (p. 36)

Layered photos (p. 35)

Coordinating papers (p. 16)

Metal embellishment

Dimensional pearl pen dots

Embossed sponged card stock (p. 39)

Hardware legs (p. 24)

Sponged edges (p. 39)

Sponged edges (p. 39)

Tools & Supplies

These following measurements are for a 10" x 7" x 2½" (254 x 178 x 64mm) box. Adjust measurements as needed to fit the one you use.

- Cigar box: approximately 10" x 7" x 2½" (254 x 178 x 64mm)

- Linen book repair tape, self-adhering: 10" x 2" (254 x 51mm), two pieces

- Metallic paint: copper

- Printed cardstock: 12" x 12" (305 x 305mm), double-sided, two matching sheets and one coordinating sheet

- Solid cardstock: 12" x 12" (305 x 305mm), brown

- Solid cardstock: 8½" x 11" (216 x 279mm), cream

- Chalk inkpads: brown, black, and green

- Embossing/die-cutting machine and texture plate

- Photos

- Pearl pen: copper

- Satin ribbon: 34" x ½" (864 x 13mm)

- Adhesive

- Copper nameplate

- Copper brads: two

- Metal embellishments

Techniques

Beautiful papers, pearl pen dots, satin ribbon, brass nameplate, layered and sponged photos, filigree metal feet, and embossed trim all combine to covert a simple, painted cigar box into a spectacular, yet functional, display piece.

Terrific tips

Use a beautiful printed paper or cardstock as part of the lid cover. You will have a gorgeous piece without breaking the bank by adding lots of embellishments.

1. Prepare the basic box. Apply linen book repair tape to the cigar box hinge, inside and out. Paint the entire box copper. Allow it to dry. Cut brown cardstock to 9¼" x 6¼" (235 x 159mm) and adhere it to the lid, centering so that the copper base shows approximately ¼" (6mm) all around. Cut printed cardstock to 9" x 6" (229 x 152mm), sponge edges with brown ink (p. 39), and adhere it in the center of the brown cardstock.

2. Create the trim. Cut a piece of printed cardstock 9" x ½" (229 x 13mm). Use a texture plate and embossing machine to add texture (p. 42).

3. Apply ink. Sponge the edges of the trim with black ink and apply ink to the embossed surface as well. Adhere trim to the box top, with the bottom of the trim approximately 1¼" (32mm) up from the bottom edge of the lid.

4. Make the nameplate. Print *Love Letters* on cream cardstock in the color of your choice. Attach to the copper nameplate, add brads, and then attach the nameplate to the box along the printed trim.

5. Layer photos. Trim photos and add light sponging around edges with green ink. Adhere to brown cardstock and trim, leaving a ½" (13mm) border on all sides. Adhere the layered photos to the box and add metal embellishment in the upper-right quadrant.

6. Cover the sides. Cut printed cardstock to equal pieces measuring 34" x 1½" (864 x 38mm). Sponge all edges with brown ink. Adhere around the sides of the box and glue ribbon to the center of all side papers.

7. Finish outside embellishments. Apply copper pearl pen dots around the lid's large, brown cardstock frame and above and below the satin ribbon. Sponge copper paint onto metal feet embellishments and adhere to box corners.

8. Finishing the inside. Cut printed cardstock to fit inside the lid. Layer photos (p. 35) onto brown cardstock and adhere inside. Print journaling and name tag on cream cardstock. Cut out on three sides and tear on the fourth. Apply brown ink, sponging edges first then applying the same pad using direct—to-paper technique (p. 39). Adhere to the inside lid. Cut printed cardstock to equal pieces measuring 34" x 1½" (864 x 38mm). Sponge all edges with brown ink. Adhere around inside of box, flush with the box bottom.

Terrific tips

To emboss a piece of cardstock that is larger than your texture plate, select a design that is very busy. Emboss half the strip, then flip it around and emboss the other end.

detail

My parents, Elsie Lucille Wilson and Jack Cofer, met while working at the Nabisco Factory in Memphis in the '40s. He worked on the mezzanine floor which overlooked where she worked on the first floor. He threw a cracker at her to get her attention and the rest is history.

He enlisted in the Army and was sent to the Phillipines as an MP as part of the cleaning up process after the war. My mother was a pro-life letter writer and since mail was slow then, Daddy received mail from home bi-weekly at best. One day, he received not just a few letters, but an entire bag of mail, all from my mother. That was about the same time he got his typical Army tattoo, a heart with her name on his upper arm.

Daddy passed away in 1977 as a result of wounds he received in WWII. My mother remained a letter writer for the rest of her life. She never forgot any birthdays of friends and relatives and all their children and even wrote letters to me, even though we both lived in the same city. These will provide material for future projects to honor my mother.

— Candace Cofer, Windham

Love Letters

Jack and Elsie, 1948

Keepsake Sewing Box

My mother-in-law, Ruth Skinner Windham, was a wonderful seamstress. She made all of her own clothes as well as the baby and toddler clothes for my husband, Larry, and our son, Michael.

She had a knack for selecting just the right fabrics and often embellished them with embroidery, exquisite lace, or covered buttons.

We have a box of her sewing supplies that I still use, although I use them in collage projects. She had a very good sense of design and bought some items, such as cards of buttons, eyelets, lace trims, and sewing essentials, which are too nice to hide in a big box in the closet. I made this box, which sits on my sewing machine cabinet, to hold them.

I finished off this project by attaching a label describing Ruth's sewing abilities, as well as a little history of the photo, inside the lid. I hope the project will become a family heirloom, handed down for generations.

RUTH SKINNER WINDHAM
Master Seamstress

Ruth Skinner Windham posed with husband Olin, and daughters Betty and Janell in front of their home in Arkansas around 1946. She made all of the girls' clothing as well as her own, then sewed baby and toddler clothes for her son Larry as well as his son Michael.

Top: Embossed die-cut aluminum photo frame and embossed aluminum nameplate.
Middle: Inked, embossed, die-cut aluminum dress forms.
Bottom: Journaling placed on the underside of the lid.

Embossed die-cut aluminum (p. 44)

Embossed aluminum (p. 42)

Sponged photo edges (p. 39)

Sponged edges (p. 39)

Nameplate (p. 36)

Metallic paint (p. 27)

Dimensional
pearl pen dots

RUTH SKINNER WINDHAM
Master Seamstress

Lace and trim (p. 22)

Thread and fiber (p. 22)

Coordinating cardstock (p. 16)

Sponged cardstock edges (p. 39)

Inked, embossed die-cut aluminum (p. 79)

Tools & supplies

- Round papier-mâché box with lid

- Printed cardstock: 12" x 12" (305 x 305mm), three sheets

- Colored aluminum sheets: 9" x 12" (229 x 305mm), two sheets

- Colored aluminum sheet scrap: 3¾" x 1¼" (95 x 32mm)

- Dress form and circle frame dies

- Texture plates: assorted

- Embossing machine

- Paintbrush

- Scissors

- Circle cutters: 2½" (64mm) and 1¾" (44mm)

- Dimensional pearl pens: lilac and black

- Embroidery thread to coordinate with paper, 1 yard (915mm) each, two colors

- Fiber to coordinate with paper: 1 yard (915mm)

- Clear-drying quick-dry adhesive

- Craft paint: metallic olive

- Cotton lace: 24" (610mm)

- Woven trim: 24" (610mm), flat

- Chalk ink

- Permanent ink

- Corner rounder punch

Techniques

Inked and embossed aluminum is striking against lovely papers covering a painted papier-mâché box. Sponged edges, layered photo and nameplate, pearl pen dots, and threads add additional texture and depth. Finish the lid in a braided trim and lace and add historical journaling inside to finish.

1. Paint and paper the box bottom.

Paint the box and lid, inside and out, with green metallic paint. Allow it to dry. Cut two pieces of printed cardstock to fit the sides, lining up the pattern where the papers meet. Be sure to leave the portion of the top that will be covered by the lid bare so that the lid will still fit correctly. Sponge edges (p. 39) with purple chalk ink.

2. Apply fiber and threads.

Mark the placement of each dress form die-cut with a pencil, top to bottom, on the box. This box required seven die-cuts, but the number will vary with the size of box. Working 4" (102mm) at a time, draw swirls and loops with glue around the middle of the box for fiber placement, then add glue and embroidery thread, one color at a time. Be sure to keep the loops and swirls centered between pencil lines where the die-cuts will be. This can be a little tricky, so keep a wooden skewer or other pointed object close at hand to help keep the threads in position. Add swirl dots with pearl pens, keeping designs between dress form pencil marks.

detail

3. Prepare die-cut dress forms.

Cut dress forms from aluminum or cardstock with a die-cutting machine (p. 44), and then emboss (p. 42) each form. Using several embossing patterns will give you variety. Rub permanent ink over the dress forms to color the raised areas (p. 37) and let them dry. Adhere dress forms to the box, centering each along pencil lines.

4. Add photo to the lid.
Cut a circle from printed cardstock slightly smaller than the lid diameter, sponge edges, and adhere it to the box lid. Emboss aluminum using a circle frame template and trim edges. Adhere it to upper-left side of the circle on the box top. Cut a 1¾" (44mm) circle from printed cardstock, sponge edges, and adhere it in the center of the aluminum frame. Cut the photo into a 2½" (64mm) circle, sponge edges, and adhere it in on top of the aluminum frame's cardstock.

5. Add a nameplate and finish.

Cut a rectangle 3¾" x 1¼" (95 x 32mm) from aluminum and emboss. Sand the raised texture for contrast. Print the nameplate label on cardstock and cut it to fit inside the embossed rectangle. Sponge edges with green ink and adhere. Attach flat cotton lace above the bottom edge of the lid and add braided trim to the top edge. Finish by adding lilac pearl dots along cardstock circle's inner edge and placing a descriptive note about the photo inside the lid.

Chapter 5
Tabletop Art Projects

Expand traditional scrapbook techniques even farther. Highlight a favorite family recipe on a serving tray (p. 82), make resin photo charms for embossed napkin rings (p. 86), and create a wonderful shadow box from two art canvases (p. 90).

Recipe Serving Tray

TEA CAKES

2 tablespoons shortening
1/2 cup sugar
1 egg
1 cup milk

3 teaspoons baking powder
2 cups flour
1 cup chopped nuts

Cream the shortening with the sugar; add the beaten egg; then add the milk alternately with the sifted ingredients. Add the floured nuts last. Bake in greased muffin pans in a moderate oven (375°F). Split each cake, butter it, and sprinkle with sugar and cinnamon or with grated maple sugar and chopped nuts. Serve with afternoon tea.

then raised all the grand kids while our mothers worked outside the home.

My sister Mary Lynn and I were the oldest grandchildren. On summer days, like the one in this photo, we played outside and only went in for a drink of water or lunch.

On winter days, we spent the indoor time coloring, drawing, singing, reading and baking.

Our favorite thing to make was Tea Cakes, from a recipe in The American Woman's Cookbook, printed in 1939. I recently made a batch of these Tea Cakes. Granny must have added some love as an extra ingredient because I can't imagine what I loved about them

Ooooohhhhh, tea cakes! I can still smell that heavenly scent coming from the big oven in Granny's kitchen. Granny allowed my sister and me to make them when we were tiny girls.

I remember her tying a big apron, which was probably a flour sack dishtowel that didn't actually protect anything, around each of us. We still ended up with flour all over us—and most of the kitchen—by the time the tea cakes went in the oven!

Granny would get all of the ingredients out of the tall kitchen cabinets for us, then supervise as we used her up-to-the-minute kitchen equipment: sifter, measuring cup (a coffee cup) and spoons (a big spoon and a little spoon), large bowl, and big stirring spoon. This was the '50s and not everyone had mixers and food processors. She would help us carefully measure everything and she always added a teaspoon of vanilla, which was not in the recipe, but usually makes most good things better.

I ran across a copy of the cookbook she used in an antique store and had to have it because hers had disappeared years ago. I have it on display in my china cabinet, opened to the tea cakes recipe.

I recently made this recipe and have no idea why I loved it so much as a child. The cakes were dry, bland, and were as hard as bricks. Still, it brings back wonderful childhood memories, so I made this tray to display beside the cookbook. The love is still there, but the tea cakes...I've had enough of those!

Do you have a favorite recipe associated with a beautiful memory? Keep the memory alive with one of these trays displayed in your kitchen or dining area. It is sure to become a treasured heirloom.

Top: Die-cut, sponged, layered nameplate.
Middle: Printed recipe with sponged edges.
Bottom: Cardstock tag with journaling.

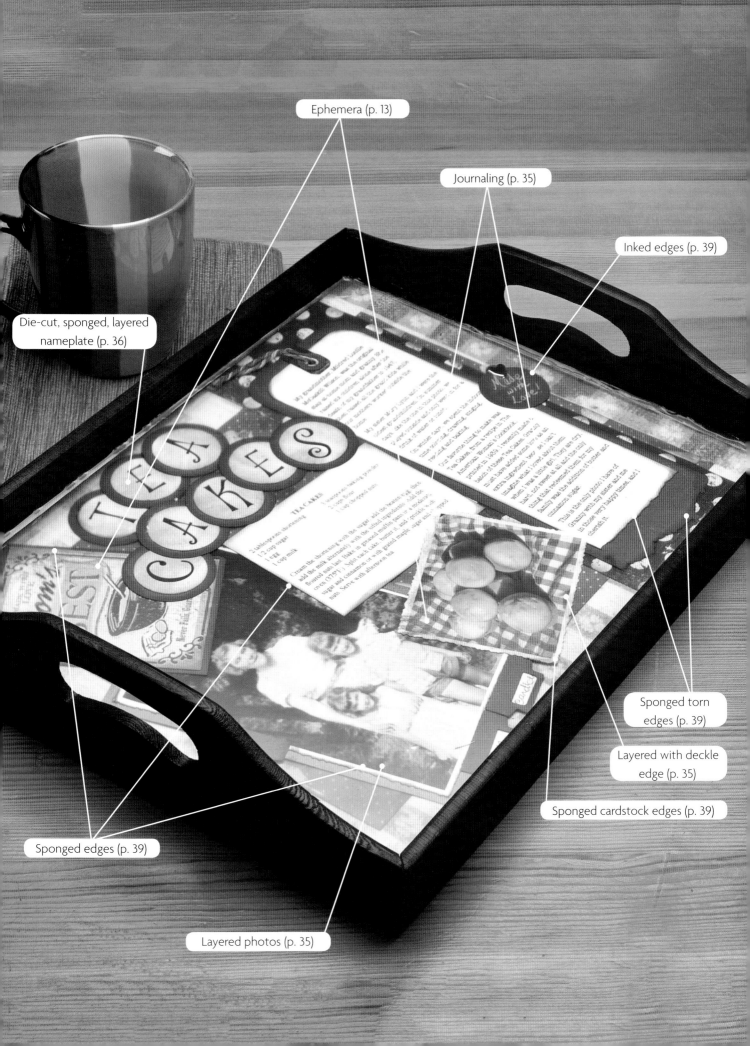

Ephemera (p. 13)

Journaling (p. 35)

Inked edges (p. 39)

Die-cut, sponged, layered
nameplate (p. 36)

Sponged torn
edges (p. 39)

Layered with deckle
edge (p. 35)

Sponged cardstock edges (p. 39)

Sponged edges (p. 39)

Layered photos (p. 35)

Tools & Supplies

- Wooden or metal tray: approximately 14" x 11" (356 x 279mm)

- Printed cardstock: 12" x 12" (305 x 305mm), two matching sheets and two coordinating sheets

- Solid cardstock to match printed papers

- Cream cardstock

- Photos

- Flat ephemera: tags, pictures of measuring spoons, or bowls, etc.

- Circle punches: 1¾" and 1½" (44 and 38mm)

- Hole punch: standard ¼" (6mm)

- Computer-generated or handwritten journaling on cream cardstock

- Embossing/die-cutting machine

- Tag die

- Dye or chalk ink: brown

- Heart-shaped brad

- Yarn: 6" (152mm), multi-colored

- Spray paint: black

- Sandpaper

- Decorative deckle-edge scissors

- Acrylic sheet cut to fit snugly inside tray

- Clear-drying, water-resistant caulk

Techniques

Inked and sponged edges on torn or deckle-edged papers contrast nicely with crisp, die-cut lettering. Photos and ephemera are layered with a variety of coordinating papers, journaling includes a favorite family recipe, and it's all protected behind a layer of clear acrylic.

1. Prepare the tray. Sand the tray to remove rough places and apply two coats of black spray paint. If your tray still feels rough, wet-sand it and apply an additional coat of black paint. Measure inside of tray bottom and trim two pieces of printed cardstock to fit. Adhere in place, matching the pattern as much as possible.

2. Print journaling. Print journaling, names, photos, title, and recipe on cream cardstock. Trim all square pieces with straight cuts except the photo of the cakes, which is trimmed with deckle-edged scissors. Sponge brown ink on all edges (p. 39).

Punch out title letters with 1½" (38mm) circle punch (p. 33). Sponge edges and tap the sponge lightly on the entire letter surface to distress it somewhat. Layer (p. 35) onto contrasting cardstock cut with 1¾" (44mm) circle punch.

TEA CAKES

2 tablespoons shortening
1/2 cup sugar
1 egg
1 cup milk

3 teaspoons baking powder
2 cups flour
1 cup chopped nuts

Cream the shortening with the sugar; add the beaten egg; then add the milk alternately with the sifted ingredients. Add the floured nuts last. Bake in greased muffin pans in a moderate oven (375°F.). Split each cake, butter it, and sprinkle with sugar and cinnamon or with grated maple sugar and chopped nuts. Serve with afternoon tea.

My grandmother, Mildred Lucille McCaskill Wilson, was the original stay-at-home mom and granny. She raised six children alone after the death of my grandfather in 1947, then raised all the grand kids while our mothers worked outside the home.

My sister Mary Lynn and I were the oldest grandchildren. On summer days, like the one in this photo, we played outside and only went in for a drink of water or lunch.

On winter days, we spent the indoor time coloring, drawing, singing, reading and baking.

Our favorite thing to make was Tea Cakes, from a recipe in The American Woman's Cookbook, printed in 1939. I recently made a batch of these Tea Cakes. Granny must have added some love as an extra ingredient because I can't imagine what I loved about them when I was a little girl. They are dry, hard, not sweet at all and the only thing that redeemed them for my family was the addition of butter and cinnamon sugar.

This is the only photo I have of Granny with my sister and me in those very happy times, and I cherish it.

3. Assemble journaling tag.

To make the journaling tag, trim a piece of solid cardstock ½" (13mm) wider and 1½" (38mm) taller than the journaling block. Round the upper corners of both pieces. Tear the bottom edge of the journaling block and sponge all the edges with brown ink. Adhere journaling block to cardstock and tear the lower edge of the cardstock. Ink all edges. Die-cut, punch, or freehand cut an oblong bar with rounded ends, approximately ½" x 2" (13 x 51mm). Wrap it front to back across the top-center of the tag with about ¾" (19mm) showing in the front. Punch a hole with a hole punch and add yarn. Cut a piece of printed cardstock 4" (102mm) wide and the height of the tray, sponge edges with brown ink, and adhere it in place. Place journaling tag on top, centering it top to bottom.

4. Add photo, recipe, and letters.

Layer the photo and recipe blocks on cardstock with ¼" (6mm) showing all around and adhere in place. Add the heart-shaped brad to a hand-written tag and glue where desired. Arrange letters across top of the tray, overlapping to fit if necessary.

5. Attach acrylic.
Place acrylic sheet in tray. Draw a thin bead of waterproof caulk around all inner edges to seal (p. 18).

Memory Charm Napkin Rings

Family gatherings are some of the most important times in our lives. Sometimes they are weekly dinners, others are monthly lunch dates, some only at holidays, and at yearly family reunions where we reconnect with relatives we haven't seen since the last family reunion. We all admire each others' children, grandchildren, and accomplishments. The talk eventually turns to those, "Do you remember when Aunt Susie..." moments.

These gatherings seem to always center around food, especially here in the south, and what better way to remind us of our loved ones who are no longer with us than a set of napkin rings with charms holding our favorite photos. This set is for a Mothers' Day luncheon and features our mothers and grandmothers.

The charm portion takes a little while to set up, but you could make a lot at one time and have them on hand for future projects. The rings themselves are quick and easy and you could make a set in less than an hour.

Make charms at least one day before you plan to make the rings. The resin has to set up overnight and won't be completely cured for three days.

Top: Photo in bezel with epoxy resin.
Middle: Stamped and embossed cardstock with ribbon detail.
Bottom: Chipboard ring covered with printed cardstock.

Layered stamped embossed paper (p. 42)

Sponged edges (p. 39)

Coordinating papers (p. 16)

Photo in bezel with epoxy resin (p. 46)

Embossing (p. 42)

Tools & Supplies for Four Rings

- Square ¾" (19mm) metal bezels (one for each napkin ring)

- Square punch: ¾" (19mm)

- Photos: print a little larger than ¾" (19mm) square

- Chipboard: 6¾" x 1¼" (171 x 32mm), one for each ring

- Printed cardstock: 12" x 12" (305 x 305mm), double-sided, two sheets

- Embossing ink: clear

- Swirl stamp

- Embossing powder: silver

- Heat tool

- Glue stick: non-wrinkling

- Ribbon: 24" (610mm), silver

- Masking tape

- Resin

- Optional: Ultra-thick embossing powder, electric skillet or griddle, and tongs or spatula

Techniques

Resin preserves precious photos in a unique way. Layered, coordinating papers are stamped and embossed with sponged edges over a chipboard base. Tie it off with silver ribbon and the table is set for a memorable event.

Terrific tips

In a hurry? Substitute ultra-thick, clear embossing powder for the resin and place charms on an electric skillet or griddle, adding additional embossing powder as it melts until it is full. Carefully remove charms from the hot surface with a pair of tongs or a spatula as they will be very hot. Transfer charms to a cool place and allow them to set for 5–10 minutes.

Embossing powder has a tendency to have air bubbles, which can be moved to the charm edge and removed with a straight pin while the material is still hot. It also will yellow with time, so if you plan to use this method, you might want to consider using gold-tone bezels instead of silver to lessen the contrast.

Terrific tips

Be sure to cut the chipboard with the grain. Test a spare piece to see how it looks when the circle is formed. If it leaves little wrinkles or waves when you curve it into a circle, cut it the opposite way.

1. Create napkin ring bases.
Form rings from chipboard and secure with masking tape on the inside of the ring. The ends should overlap about ¼" (6mm).

2. Cover the base ring. Cut printed cardstock to 7" x 3" (178 x 76mm). Apply non-wrinkling adhesive to the chipboard ring. Center printed cardstock so that you have about an inch overlap on each side of the ring. Press cardstock to secure. Cut overlapped cardstock into tabs on each side about every ¼" (6mm). Apply adhesive to the underside of the tabs and fold to the inside.

Cut an additional piece of cardstock 7" x 1" (178 x 25mm) and adhere, with the opposite printed side out, to the inside of the ring for a finished look. Begin the inside piece of cardstock about 1½" (38mm) from the seam created when you joined the chipboard ends to help secure the ring shape.

3. Emboss top layer. Cut cardstock 7½" x 1" (191 x 25mm). With the same side up as the first ring cover, apply ink to the paper to darken (p. 39). Pat the strip down with anti-static powder. Stamp swirls in clear embossing ink. Sprinkle on silver embossing powder, remove the excess, and heat with heat tool until set (p. 47). Polish with a soft cloth or paper towel to remove excess ink and reveal the embossed image. Apply adhesive to the bottom of the strip and wrap it around the ring, centering from side to side.

4. Attach ribbon and charms.
Tie silver ribbon around the ring and tie with a knot. Slip a charm onto the ribbon and finish with a bow.

detail

Shadow Box Book

I love gallery-wrapped canvas, especially the thick ones. I have a big box of them just waiting for me to come up with the next wonder of the modern world. These days, though, I am more interested in looking back at events and people who influenced me and made me what I am today.

This piece is a tribute to my sisters-in-law, Janell and Betty Windham. Betty was the older of the two and apparently the more serious. Janell was good at getting into trouble.

This piece can be displayed on a bookshelf or table and the subject matter is endless: children, parents, aunts and uncles, grandchildren, office friends...I think I know what everyone is getting for Christmas this year!

Top: Canvases with painted and sanded edges, attached with hinges.
Middle: Photo with sponged edges.
Bottom: Hinge detail.

Die-cut letters (p. 44)

Torn tag with sponged edges (p. 39)

Torn dictionary journaling with sponged edges (p. 35)

Sponged edges (p. 39)

Black foil trim

Metal tag with punched letters, alcohol ink, and wax metallic finish (p. 26)

Tools & Supplies

- Gallery-wrapped canvas: 7¾" x 10" x 2" (197 x 254 x 51mm)

- Acrylic craft paint

- Clear-drying adhesive

- Cream cardstock: 8½" x 11" (216 x 279mm), two sheets

- Black cardstock scrap: 4" x 5½" (102 x 140mm)

- Patterned cardstock: 12" x 12" (305 x 305mm), double-sided, coordinating patterns, five sheets

- Alphabet printed cardstock: 12" x 12" (305 x 305mm), one sheet

- Shipping tag

- Rubber background stamps

- Permanent inkpad: black

- Chalk inkpads: brown, blue, and coral

- Solid cardstock

- Ink-jet photo prints

- Silk or paper flowers

- Small glass bottles

- Ephemera or embellishments of your choice

- Foil trim: 24" (610mm), black

- Embossing machine

- Texture plates

- Computer-generated quote

- Dictionary page containing definition of "sister"

- Paper lace doilies: two 3½" (89mm)

- Round metal tag

- Metal alphabet embossing dies

- Jeweler's hammer

- Metal block

- Leather pad

- Small sponge

- Cutting machine and alphabet, or chipboard letters

- Adhesive

- Sandpaper or sanding block

- Round flower punch 1¾" (44mm)

- Tag punch or die and die-cutting machine

- Assorted photos

- Hinges, two

- Clasp

- Wax metallic finish

- Decorative push pin

- Small safety pin

Techniques

Apply some paint, layer with coordinating papers and embossed cardstock, then add die-cut photos, backgrounds, and lettering with sponged edges. Trim with black foil trim, add a journaling tag, ephemera, and hammered metal tag, and you have a wonderful dedication piece.

Terrific tips

If you don't have a dictionary you can tear, copy the definition onto cream cardstock.

A sister
is a
little bit of
childhood
that can
never
be lost.
– Marion C. Garretty

BETTY

detail

COVERS

1. Paint canvases. Paint both canvases, front and back, with acrylic paint and allow them to dry. Sponge brown ink along all edges (p. 39). Lightly sand off paint in some areas to age as desired (p. 21).

2. Front cover. Cut cream cardstock ½" (13mm) smaller all around than the canvas front. Ink edges and adhere to the canvas. Cut patterned paper ⅛" (3mm) smaller all around than the cream cardstock. Sponge edges with brown ink, center on the cardstock, and adhere. Cut out a photo, sponge the edges, and adhere it to the right side of the cover.

3. "Sisters" tag. Cut letters from patterned cardstock with a cutting machine or adhere cardstock to painted chipboard letters and trim. Sponge edges with brown ink and layer the letters onto a cream cardstock strip 7¾" x 1½" (197 x 38mm). Sponge edges of the strip.

Cut patterned cardstock to 8½" x 2" (216 x 51mm), sponge edges, and adhere to the *Sisters* strip, centering. Cut additional cream cardstock 8¾" x 2⅜" (222 x 60mm), sponge edges, and adhere the entire *Sisters* tag to it. Do not adhere the tag to the canvas yet.

Using a jeweler's hammer and block, pound a metal circle tag to distress it.

Use alphabet dies to hammer names onto the tag (p. 42). Apply alcohol ink to the letters, allowing the ink to run into crevices on the tag. Wipe off excess ink then apply wax metallic finish (p. 41). Add a heart charm and jump ring. Punch two small holes in the *Sisters* tag and tie the tag and charm to the tag with a brown cord. Adhere the *Sisters* tag to the canvas cover then add black foil trim around the tag's edge.

4. Definition tag. Tear or cut definition of "sister" from a dictionary page and ink the edges with brown ink. Trim a shipping tag to 4¾" x 1¾" (121 x 44mm). Score the tag 1" (25mm) from the hanging edge. Fold so that the stringed flap is on top. Adhere the definition to the tag and attach it to the canvas cover.

5. Alphabet trim. Cut printed alphabet cardstock to 12" x 1" (305 x 25mm). Sponge edges and adhere, centering around both canvas sides.

INSIDE, LEFT SIDE

6. Background. Trim patterned cardstock to fit the background and glue in place. Ink edges of paper doilies with brown ink and adhere them to the background paper inside the frame.

detail

7. Photo montages. Cut two 2¾" (70mm) circles from patterned cardstock. Punch two round flowers from photos and two round flowers from patterned cardstock. Center each photo on a round flower and adhere all to a 2¾" (70mm) circle, then to the lace doilies.

Write names on cream cardstock and adhere them to patterned cardstock scraps. Add black trim and a brad to left side of each and attach to their respective photos. Sponge edges of tickets with brown ink and pin together with a small safety pin. Glue to the background paper.

8. Sentiment quote. Print the sentiment in brown ink on cream cardstock and punch out with a tag die cutter or large punch, centering the text. Stamp swirly flowers in brown ink along the bottom of the tag. Sponge edges with coral and brown inks. Adhere the tag to a patterned paper scrap and carefully trim to the same shape as the tag, leaving a ⅛" (3mm) edge all around. Punch a hole in the top of the tag and thread ribbon through it using a lark's head knot (p. 51). Punch a small hole in the center of the tag bottom and, using a jump ring, attach a heart charm. Suspend the sentiment quote from the top inside of the canvas with a small, decorative pushpin.

9. Finish frame edges. Cut strips of patterned cardstock to equal 24" x 1" (102 x 140mm) and adhere around the inside frame edge. Adhere jacks and ball on the frame ledge with quick-dry adhesive. Cut a frame from patterned cardstock ½" (13mm) smaller all around than the inner and outer canvas edges. Sponge with coral, blue, and brown inks and adhere to the canvas.

Life is not perfect.
That's why
we have sisters.

PLAYMATES
A PRIM

detail

INSIDE, RIGHT SIDE

10. Background. Trim patterned cardstock to fit inside the canvas frame and adhere to the background.

11. Layer the photo. Cut contrasting patterned cardstock to 4" x 5½" (102 x 140mm). Tear the right edge and ink all edges with brown ink.

Emboss black cardstock with embossing machine and texture plate (p. 42). Tear approximately ½" (13mm) from the right side of the embossed black cardstock and adhere it to the printed cardstock. Add a photo and adhere all layers to the background paper.

12. Add ephemera. Cut out childhood book images, sponge their edges, and adhere them to the lower center of the frame (p. 39). Adhere dried flowers on the left side and letterpress letters to the right. Tie hemp through buttons, sponge edges of puzzle pieces, and adhere all to the background cardstock.

13. Create the sentiment: Print a sentiment on cream cardstock, trim it to fit in the nameplate (p. 36), and sponge edges. Adhere it to the nameplate, add brads to each side, and glue to the background cardstock over the layered photo.

14. Finish frame edges. Finish the inside frame and frame edges the same as the left side.

15. Add hardware and signature. With canvas insides facing each other, attach hinges to the left side of the book and a clasp to right side, if desired. You may want to decorate the back cover. I use this area to sign and date the piece with a permanent, fine-point marker.

Chapter 6
Bonus Projects

Kick it up a notch with these three bonus projects. The techniques are the same, but the media varies. Make a book from scratch (p. 98), turn metal into a beautiful plant hanger (p. 104), and stitch up a photo wall hanging (p. 110). The possibilities are endless.

Happy Birthday!

D TO BE AN
ERICAN

USA

Birthday Card Book

Don't you just love receiving cards, especially in this digital age when it's so much easier to just hit the send button? Going to the store, finding exactly the right card, writing a nice note, then addressing the card, stamping it, and carrying it to the mailbox means a lot. I know I appreciate a beautiful greeting card and am very fortunate to have lots of friends who create handmade cards. Receiving cards lets me know they cared enough to take the time for me.

I have to admit that my hubby just doesn't understand why I have to keep every card I receive, including Christmas cards, from year to year. To me, they are a fun way to revisit the past.

Of course, storing them in a box in the attic is not very practical. If you want to revisit them, you have to climb the stairs and dig through boxes, so it doesn't happen very often. That's why I came up with this design to hold my card collection and it fits quite nicely on a bookshelf.

Top: Printed cardstock for interior book liner.
Middle: Ribbon binding holds cards of all sizes.
Bottom: Journaling with sponged edges placed in a die-cut nameplate.

Sponged book tape (p. 19)

Coordinating papers (p. 16)

Ribbon binding holds cards

Dimensional pearl pen dots

Dresden foil trim

Die-cut nameplate (p. 44)

Happy Birthday!

Ephemera (p. 13)

Sponged edges (p. 39)

Layering (p. 35)

Journaling (p. 35)

Sponged cardstock edges (p. 39)

Tools & Supplies

- Mat board, book board, or heavy chipboard: 9" x 12" (229 x 305mm)

- Printed cardstock: 12" x 12" (305 x 305mm), double-sided, three sheets

- Cream cardstock scrap

- Trim: 20" (508mm), Dresden foil or lace

- Ribbon: ⅛" (3mm) wide, 10 yards (914cm)

- Ribbon: 2" (51mm) wide, 12" (305mm) each, two pieces

- Gold leafing pen

- Computer-generated title

- Metal nameplate

- Tyveck: 5" x 9" (127 x 229mm)

- Embellishments of your choice

- Wood skewers: ⅛" (3mm) diameter

- Canvas book tape: 2" x 11" (51 x 279mm), two pieces

- Inkpad to blend with printed paper on cover

Techniques

Mat board has never looked better. Covered by beautiful, coordinating papers; simple shading; an ornate, layered, die-cut nameplate; and Dresden foil, strength becomes beautiful. It's all held together by sponged canvas book tape decorated with pearl pen dots. Add ribbon and it's a keepsake for the ages.

MAKING THE COVERS

Cut mat board to two 6" x 9" (152 x 229mm) pieces for the front and back covers and one 2" x 9" (51 x 229mm) piece for the spine. Cut cardstock into two 7" x 10" (178 x 254mm) pieces for the outside cover.

1. Scoring. Place outside cover cardstock face down. Apply adhesive to the mat board, centering it on the cover pieces. Use a bone folder to score around the edges of the cardstock (p. 28) following the mat board as a guide for a clean fold. Use the bone folder to disperse the glue evenly for a smooth cover surface.

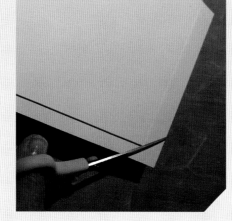

2. Trimming. Cut the corners off at 45° angles to create mitered corners on the inside. Be careful to not trim too close to the corners. Cutting within ⅛" (3mm) from the corner is sufficient. Apply adhesive and fold cardstock to the inside of each cover.

3. Correcting errors. If you accidently overcut your corner, mat board will show through after folding. Most of this will be hidden by the inside covers but you may wish to use one of the corners you cut off to hide the error.

ASSEMBLING THE BOOK

4. Straight and even. Place finished book covers on either side of the spine, right sides down, on a flat surface. Keep ⅛" (3mm) space on either side of the spine. Wooden kitchen skewers placed between the covers and spine are the perfect spacers for adhering Tyveck.

Terrific tips

Those indestructible Tyveck envelops you receive in the mail make indestructible binding for your books. It doesn't matter if it has printing on it, because it will be covered.

5. Strengthening. Adhere Tyveck, centering and smoothing over the spine. When dry, flip the book so outside covers and bare spine are face up. Ink/paint two strips of canvas book tape to coordinate with the cover. Attach tape to front and back, centering top to bottom and side to side, with ¼" (6mm) overlapping on each side of the cover. Repeat inside.

6. Inside covers. Trim additional printed cardstock to 5" x 9" (127 x 229mm). Adhere to the inside spine, centering right to left. Attach 2" (51mm)-wide ribbon with strong adhesive to left and right inside covers, centering top to bottom. Cut two pieces of cardstock 5¾" x 8¾" (146 x 222mm), adhere to front and back inside covers, and smooth with a bone folder.

EMBELLISH AND ATTACH RIBBON

7. Pretty and personal. Create a nameplate (p. 36). Add brads (decorative only) and attach nameplate to the cover with strong adhesive. Adhere foil trim along edges where different papers overlap at front and back. Apply dots along book tape on front and back outside covers with a dimensional pearl pen. Let dry.

8. Ribbon cardholders. Wrap a roll of ⅛" (3mm) ribbon around the spine. Knot at the top, glue the knot to secure, and do not cut. Continue wrapping ribbon around the spine and along it's width until you come to the end of the roll. Bring the last 18" (457mm) to the top of the book. Tie a bow with each ribbon end.

9. Smallest in front. Slip cards into the book by sliding them onto the ribbon on the inside. Arrange with the smallest cards in front so they don't get lost among their larger counterparts.

Terrific tips

A standard roll of ⅛" (3mm) ribbon typically yields about 20 loops on the spine. If you prefer to add more, tie the end of the first spool to the beginning of the new spool, leaving the knot on the inside of the spine.

detail

Copper Flower Hanger

I remember my grandmother and her neighbors trading cuttings from their flower beds and gardens. There would be a row of canning jars or jelly glasses lined up on the windowsill, waiting for the roots to appear. At times, especially early spring when the windows were opened in the morning and closed at night, the cuttings got in the way and were in danger of landing on the counter or lying in a puddle.

I had some test tubes left over from an older project and a plant my sister gave me years ago with the advice, "You can't kill it." She was right. I have given away so many cuttings from this plant and generally have several pieces rooting at any given time. Now my hubby is the one fussing about the jars in the window, so I came up with this lovely holder to honor my great-grandmother while being practical as well.

Top: Die-cut nameplate and clay flowers with metallic paint.
Middle: Layered photo with sponged edges and ephemera detail.
Bottom: Glass vials with copper foil tape detailing.

Embossed copper tape (p. 42)

Test tubes

Inked leaves (p. 25)

Clay flower and petals (p. 45)

Embossed inked copper (p. 42)

Ephemera (p. 13)

Painted nameplate (p. 36)

Layered photo with sponged edges (p. 39)

Tools & Supplies

- Copper mesh: 8" x 12" (203 x 305mm)

- Wire: 16 gauge, 24" (610mm)

- Air-dry clay

- Mat board scrap: cut into a tag shape

- Ink jet photo

- Test tubes: available at school and medical supply companies

- Copper tape: ⅜" x 10" (10 x 254mm)

- Copper sheeting: 10" x 2" (254 x 51mm), four strips

- Texture plate and embossing machine of your choice

- Metal embellishments of your choice

- Copper metallic acrylic paint

- Clear-drying adhesive

- Heavy-duty, clear-drying adhesive

- Heavy-duty ⅛" (3mm) hole punch (Cropadile)

- Eyelet

- Hemp cord or chain, 24" (610mm)

- Assorted beads

- Wire cutters

- Eye wires

- Jump rings

Techniques

Metal becomes beautiful when it's embossed, folded, and inked. Gold-trimmed glass test tubes glisten in the wire mesh pocket adorned with beads, painted clay flowers, an ornate nameplate, and a sponged photo.

Terrific tips

When attaching metal embellishments to the pocket, place waxed paper inside the pocket before applying adhesive to keep it from running through to the back.

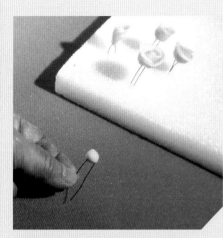

1. Copper stems. Cut copper wire into 4" (102mm) pieces. Fold wire in half and insert the looped end into a small ball of clay for the stem portion.

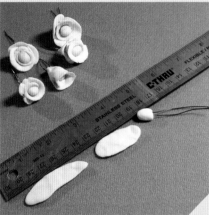

2. Making petals. Roll clay pieces until they are approximately ½" (13mm) wide and lengths between ½" (38mm) and 2" (51mm) for petals.

3. Securing. Wrap petal pieces around the stem piece, squeezing slightly at the base to secure. Add petals to create several flowers of various sizes and let them air dry.

4. Painting flowers. When dry, paint the flowers with copper metallic acrylic and let them dry. For added depth, brush dark brown acrylic over the dry copper paint and immediately wipe it away for an antiqued effect. Add alcohol ink to the leaves to highlight and emphasize details.

5. Mesh pocket. Fold wire mesh to make a pocket 8" x 7" (203 x 178mm). It's easier to make the fold in the wire mesh if you fold it over a metal ruler.

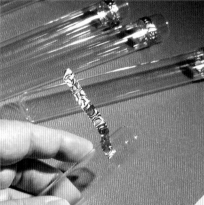

6. Embossing copper. Emboss copper sheeting strips and copper tape. Apply tape around top of each test tube.

7. Alcohol inks. Use a felt applicator or piece of cut felt and alcohol ink to change the color of your metal. After adding texture by embossing, place three colors of alcohol ink on the felt pad and repeatedly press it to the metal copper sheeting strips in a random pattern. Continue until the metal is colored to your liking. Let it dry.

8. Attachments. Push clay flower wires through the wire mesh pocket from the front and twist on the inside of the pocket until stable. Print the photo onto parchment paper and adhere it to the mat board tag, punch a hole in the top with a heavy-duty hole punch, and tie it to the pocket front with hemp.

9. Stitching sides. Stitch pocket sides together with 16-gauge wire. Insert short pieces of copper wire through the pocket front and back at the sides and twist to keep them closed. Attach two pieces of copper sheeting to the back top of the pocket and adhere with strong adhesive.

10. Attach sides. Fold remaining two pieces of copper sheeting in half to make strips 10" x 1" (254 x 25mm). Adhere one to the top fold of the wire pouch with heavy-duty adhesive, then cut the remaining copper sheeting strip in half, apply heavy-duty adhesive, and use pieces to cover stitches on the sides.

11. Additions. Paint the metal nametag gold and let it dry. Hand-letter cardstock for the nametag. Attach the nametag and any other embellishments to the pocket with heavy-duty adhesive. String beads onto eye wires and hang them along the bottom of the pocket with jump rings.

12. Ready to hang. Insert large eyelets at each corner. Insert test tubes into the pocket. Add a hemp tie or chain to hang in the window with your own cuttings or fresh flowers from your garden.

Fabric Photo Wall Hanging

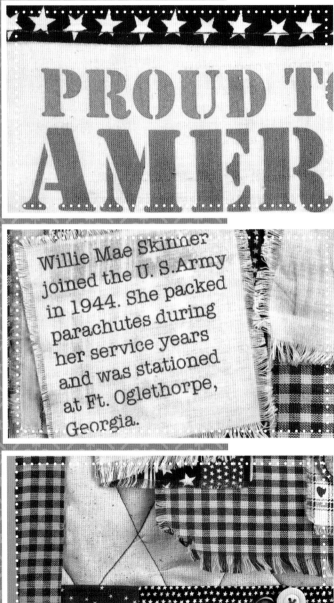

All branches of our family have had a history of patriotism, whether they were serving in the armed forces or keeping up the home front. We have been great heroes and career soldiers, and there were several who made the ultimate sacrifice.

I was touched by the story of my husband's Aunt Willie Mae Skinner. During World War II, her father was deemed unfit for military service and it broke his heart. Willie Mae promptly enlisted in his place as an honor to him.

This project is my tribute to her. It's quick and easy and can be made from scraps you may have in your fabric stash. I wanted an Americana look so I chose patriotic prints then added brown chalk ink from a stamp pad to give it a rustic look.

Top: Ink-jet printed fabric.
Middle: Journaling printed on fabric with frayed edges.
Bottom: Fabric strips with button detailing.

Hanging tabs

Top border strip

Journaling (p. 35)

Title block bands

Inked edges (p. 25)

Title block

Ephemera (p. 13)

Ink-jet printed fabric (p. 114)

Sponged edges (p. 39)

Side strip

Journaling (p. 35)

PROUD TO BE AN
AMERICAN

★ WILLIE
MAE
SKINNER

Willie Mae Skinner
joined the U. S. Army
in 1944. She packed
parachutes during
her service years
and was stationed
at Ft. Oglethorpe,
Georgia.

Side strip

Quilted muslin

Layered fabric with frayed edges

Stamped cork in bottle caps (p. 37)

Bottom border strip

Tools & Supplies

- Coordinating printed cotton fabric, ginghams, and Americana prints: ¼ yard (229mm) each

- Muslin: ½ yard (457mm)

- Quilt batting

- Perfect Crafting Anti-Static Pouch

- Ink jet printer

- Sewing machine

- Sewing thread, cotton: red and cream

- Scissors

- Military or patriotic ephemera: star brads, old military pins, etc.

- Decorative rod

- Assorted buttons: eight red, white, and blue

- Chalk ink: dark brown

- Iron-on adhesive

- Iron

- Fabric adhesive

- Freezer paper

Techniques

Fabric can be used just like paper: printed, layered, and sponged. Add texture with quilting and frayed edges. You can print photos on it, create journaling, and add buttons, bottle caps, and ephemera. Then, hang it on the wall for all to see.

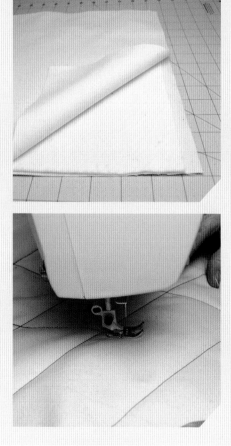

1. Muslin and batting. Cut two pieces of muslin 13½" x 21" (330 x 533mm). Cut one piece of quilt batting 13½" x 20¼" (330 x 514mm). Place quilt batting between the two pieces of muslin, aligning at the top so that the batting is shorter than the muslin on the bottom (Figure 1, p. 115).

2. Quilt the panel. Machine quilt in a harlequin pattern with red cotton thread, leaving 1½" (38mm) of the muslin unquilted on top and bottom edges (Figure 1, p. 115). Don't worry if the lines aren't perfectly straight. Most of this will be covered and uneven stitches give a handmade look.

3. Border strips. Cut four strips 13" x 2" (330 x 51mm) from patterned fabric. Fold in seam allowances ½" (13mm), apply iron-on adhesive or fabric glue, and attach to the top front of the quilted fabric (Figure 2, p. 116). Add another strip at the base approximately ¾" (19mm) from the bottom edge. Add buttons. Save two strips for title block top and bottom.

(Figure 2, p. 116)

4. Side strips. Cut two strips of gingham fabric 3" x 21" (76 x 533mm). Turn and press sides in ½" (13mm), then fold in half vertically (Figure 4, p.116). Turn top of each strip in ½" (13mm) and secure with fabric glue.

(Figure 4, p.116)

Terrific tips

If you do not like the stitches of each piece showing on the back, do not add your side strips until everything is stitched in place, then add a piece of plain muslin to the back. Turn the top edge under and secure with iron-on adhesive or fabric glue, then add side strips.

For a more handmade look, stitch the layered fabrics to the background by hand.

To give the fabric an aged appearance, fray all raw edges and stamp or sponge edges with brown ink.

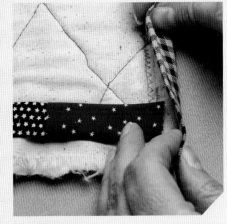

5. Attaching. Turn top muslin edges in ½" (13mm) but leave open for the tabs. Apply iron-on adhesive or fabric glue to long edges of both strips. Attach strips to each side of the quilted backing, turning and pressing into place. Trim lower portions of gingham and quilted muslin straight across the bottom. Ravel ½" (13mm) of all bottom edges of fabrics.

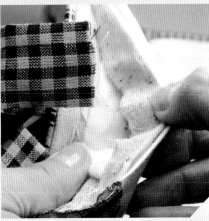

6. Hanging tabs. Cut five pieces of gingham (Figure 2, p. 116) 3" x 6" (76 x 152mm). Stitch, right sides together. Turn and press leaving ends open. Ravel one end ½" (13mm). Insert the other end into the top edge between muslin, seams facing forward. Space tabs evenly. Stitch the seam closed. Fold tabs to the front and stitch buttons in place to secure.

(Figure 2, p. 116)

Mae Skinner
the U. S. Army
4. She packed
utes during
rvice years
s stationed
glethorpe,
.

7. Printing. Cut freezer paper to 8½" x 11" (216 x 279mm) sheets. Line up paper edges with the grain of the fabric. Iron muslin to the shiny side of the freezer paper. Trim to paper edges. Dust fabric with an anti-static embossing pouch to prevent bleeding. Print titles and photo on an inkjet printer. Remove freezer paper.

8. Attach title block. Trim the title block and title block strips from Step 3 to 9" (229mm) wide. Ravel ends. Overlap strips on top and bottom edges of the title block and top stitch along the fold to attach. Top stitch outer folded edges of title block strips. Attach strip-edged title block to the background with fabric glue or iron-on adhesive.

9. Hanging. Cut additional print fabric to 8" x 12" (208 x 305mm), 3¼" x 9½" (83 x 241mm), and 3" x 4" (76 x 102mm). Trim and ravel all edges of the muslin. Place according to the photo. Secure with iron-on adhesive or fabric glue, layering printed text and photos on top. Embellish as desired.

Quilt to within 1½" (38mm) of top border

Figure 1

Fabric Panel Base
Enlarge 200%

Cut two muslin pieces.

Cut one quilt batting piece, ¾" (19mm) shorter on the bottom.

Quilt to within 1½" (38mm) of bottom border

Cutting line for quilt batting

½"

Fabric Strips, Top and Bottom

½" Seam (13mm) Allowance

2" (51mm)

13" (330mm)

Cut four strips from different fabric patterns, one for top, one for bottom. and two for title block.

Trim title block strips to 9" (229mm) wide.

Fold in seam allowance on top and bottom borders and attach to upper background with iron-on adhesive or fabric glue.

Note: Do not stitch the top border in place. The upper portion of the quilted piece needs to remain open to accept the tabs. The iron-on adhesive or fabric glue will hold it securely.

Fold in ½" (13mm) at top

Cut two strips from gingham fabric, one for each side

Figure 2

Fabric Border Strips, Top, Bottom and Tabs

½"

Figure 4

Fabric Border Strips, Sides

Tab

½" (13mm)

½" (13mm)

Insert into top of background ½" (13mm).

Top Tabs

Cut five from patterned fabric.

6" (152mm)

½" (13mm) Seam Allowance

½" (13mm) Seam Allowance

3" (76mm)

Fray bottom edge to ½" (13mm).

Fold Line

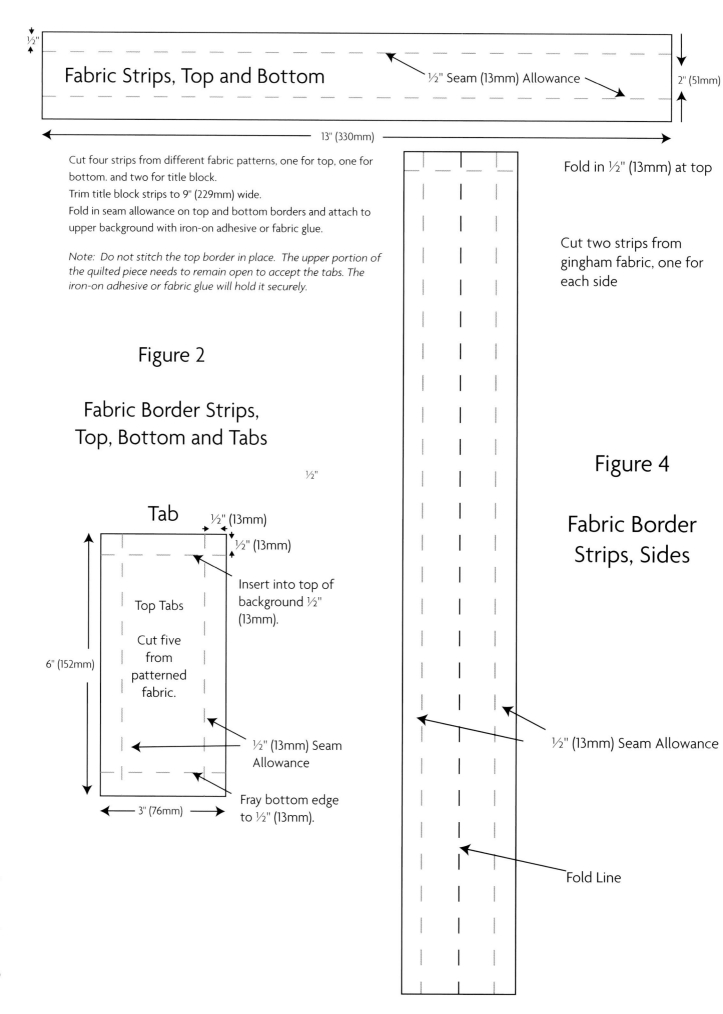

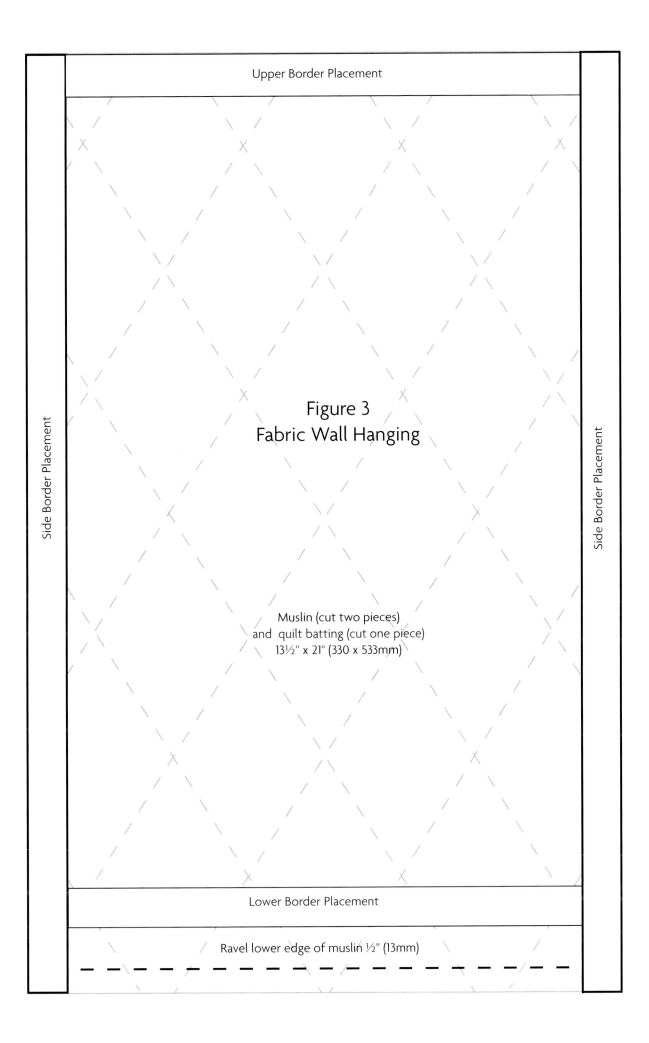

Upper Border Placement

Side Border Placement

Side Border Placement

Figure 3
Fabric Wall Hanging

Muslin (cut two pieces)
and quilt batting (cut one piece)
13½" x 21" (330 x 533mm)

Lower Border Placement

Ravel lower edge of muslin ½" (13mm)

Contributor acknowledgments:

You can purchase these products at your local craft store. Special thanks to the following vendors who contributed materials for the projects in this book.

ScraPerfect

Sizzix

Viva Décor

ACQUISITION EDITOR: Peg Couch

ASSISTANT EDITOR: Katie Weeber

ASSOCIATE EDITOR: Kerri Landis

COPY EDITOR: Paul Hambke

COVER AND LAYOUT DESIGNER: Ashley Millhouse

COVER AND GALLERY PHOTOGRAPHER: Scott Kriner

DEVELOPMENTAL EDITOR: Debbie Henry

PROOFREADER: Lynda Jo Runkle

INDEXER: Jay Kreider

Index

More Great Books from Design Originals

Stash & Smash
ISBN 978-1-57421-409-3 **$16.99**
DO5380

Pulp Fiction, 2nd Edition
ISBN 978-1-57421-413-0 $16.99
DO5384

Steampunk Your Wardrobe
ISBN 978-1-57421-417-8 **$19.99**
DO5388

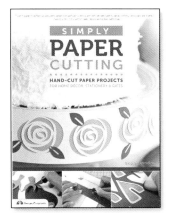

Simply Paper Cutting
ISBN 978-1-57421-418-5 **$19.99**
DO5389

Vision Box Idea Book
ISBN 978-1-57421-407-9 **$16.99**
DO5378

Banners, Swags and Pennants for Every Occasion
ISBN 978-1-57421-348-5 **$8.99**
DO3471

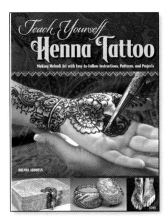

Teach Yourself Henna Tattoo
ISBN 978-1-57421-417-7 **$19.99**
DO5385

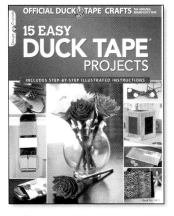

Official Duck Tape® Crafts
ISBN 978-1-57421-350-8 **$8.99**
DO3473

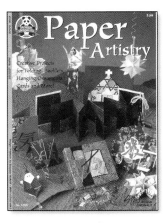

Paper Artistry
ISBN 978-1-57421-498-7 **$12.99**
DO5188